iPhone XS Guide

1st edition 2018
Published by Tap Guides Ltd
Contact: mail@tapguides.co.uk

Written by Tom Rudderham

Contents

Before we begin...

Download your free eBook

Because you're such a wonderful person and purchased this book in print, you're entitled to also download the Kindle eBook edition for free. While a print version is brilliant for reference, looks great on a shelf, and is nice to flick through, the eBook edition also has:

- Color Images.
- Automatic book updates direct to your eBook reading device.
- Better portability.

Here's how you can grab the Kindle edition:

1. Go to **Manage Your Content and Devices**.
2. Select the **Settings** tab.
3. Under **Automatic Book Update**, select **On**.
4. Note: If you select Off, you will no longer receive book updates automatically.

Have a question?

If you have a question about your iPhone that isn't covered in this book, then please get in touch using the email address below. I'll personally reply with a solution ASAP, and also include the answer in future editions of this book: **mail@tapguides.co.uk**

Introduction

The iPhone has been in the hands of consumers for more than a decade, and during that time has become one of the most recognizable pieces of technology available to buy. You could almost call it a cultural icon.

Since its initial launch in 2007, it has redefined the computer industry, and changed the lives of billions of people, thanks to its innovative operating system and incredible App Store. It's now eleven years since the launch of the iPhone, and the pace of its development is yet to slow down. As this book goes to press, the iPhone Xs and Xs Max are beginning to ship to customers. They include faster processors, better cameras, more refined software, and for those who purchase the Max model, the largest screens ever shipped on an iPhone.

This book is here to help you understand the iPhone, from its very basics — such as setting up Wi-Fi — to it's most advanced features, like using the Home app to control the lights and smart appliances within your home. You'll also learn about the history of the iPhone, its operating system, what to do if you have a hardware problem, plus much more.

A brief history of the iPhone

You might not know it, but the iPhone in your pocket is the most advanced piece of technology in the history of the world.

It's crammed with sensors, antennas, a fingernail-sized CPU, three camera systems, wireless charging... the list is nearly endless; but it's the software that really elevates the iPhone above any other piece of technology. It can scan your face in an instant, analyze the world around you, capture that world, understand your voice and tone, your movements, your habits; and it has access to millions of third-party apps that unlock an endless list of possibilities.

Perhaps what's most incredible is that this amazing handheld computer is used by millions of people around the globe. Millions of people who intuitively know how to use its user interface, who trust the device with their personal information, and who can afford to purchase the hardware. The iPhone isn't limited to the ultra rich, nor does it require training in any capacity to understand. It's a device for the masses, and it has transformed the world since its release in 2007.

iPhone X is the cumulative result of more than a decade of development, and it's the most advanced version of the most advanced device on the planet. To understand how we got to this point, let's journey back to 2007 and take a quick look at the history of the iPhone.

2007: iPhone

The world was a different place in 2007. The mobile industry was dominated by Nokia and Blackberry, while technology pundits were predicting Microsoft to be the dominant force in the years to come. Most people used their mobiles to call and text friends and family. A few took low-resolution photos. Even fewer used their phones to browse the web.

Looking back a decade later, it's obvious that 2007 was the year when the internet changed forever. It was when Twitter and Facebook began to take off, when AirBnB was dreamed up, when YouTube became truly massive. It was also the year that the iPhone was launched.

At the time, many were confused by the iPhone. They saw it as too expensive, they saw the lack of a removable battery as a backward step; and they thought the Multi-Touch keyboard was a terrible idea.

They were all missing the bigger picture, because the iPhone was the first truly handheld computer, and it made the web accessible from anywhere in the world, at any time, and in any situation. It was the moment when people became truly connected to one another, no matter where they were; and it all started with these famous words: "...a widescreen iPod with touch controls, a revolutionary mobile phone and a breakthrough internet communications device. An iPod... a phone... and an internet communicator. An iPod, a phone... are you getting it? These are not three separate devices. This is one device! And we are calling it: iPhone. Today, Apple is going to reinvent the phone."

Those words were spoken by Steve Jobs as he announced iPhone to the world. The audience went wild. They whooped and hollered for a product they hadn't even seen yet.

Over the next hour, Steve demoed the iPhone to a captivated crowd. No one had ever seen Multi-Touch before or even thought about the idea of scrolling through lists with a finger. By the end of that morning, Apple had completely revolutionized the entire mobile phone industry. Its rivals were left in disbelief, and in public, they scrambled to play down its significance. Mike Lazaridis, CEO of Blackberry at the time said: "Try typing a web key on a touchscreen on an Apple iPhone, that's a real challenge; you cannot see what you type." Microsoft CEO, Steve Balmer, laughed on camera while remarking: "Five hundred dollars fully subsidized with a plan! I said that is the most expensive phone in the world and it doesn't appeal to business customers because it doesn't have a keyboard, which makes it not a very good email machine."

In hindsight, these comments seem absurd, but at the time they were real concerns. Nevertheless, during the course of 2007 more than 1.4 million iPhones were sold around the world, kicking off a revolution that changed the world.

2008: iPhone 3G

This was a year that kicked off a chain of events that ruined lives for millions of people. Thankfully we're not talking about a new iPhone. We're talking about the Stock Market crash, which led to a global recession that seemed to last an eon.

As this series of terrible events began to unfurl, the iPhone 3G was announced at

WWDC on June 9th. It was twice as fast as the earlier model and half the price. It featured the same 3.5-inch screen, but received a significant update to its wireless radio: support for 3G UMTS, and it also came with a plastic shell that felt warmer in the hand. Just as important were the software updates: the iPhone would 3G would launch alongside the App Store, enabling users to install third-party apps; MobileMe was introduced, which synced emails, calendars, and contacts across devices, and there was the introduction of Street View to the Maps app.

Maybe 2008 wasn't so bad after all.

2009: iPhone 3GS

It was the year that Barack Obama was inaugurated as the 44th President of the United States. It was also the year that the iPhone 3GS was revealed, which sported an even faster processor, 3-megapixel camera with video recording capabilities, digital compass and support for 7.2 Mbit/s HSDPA downloading.

Alongside improved internal hardware, the iPhone 3GS was released with iPhone OS 3, which included a long-awaited copy and paste function, spotlight for searching content on the device, MMS for sending photos and video clips via the Messages app, and Push Notifications for alerting the user when new emails, tweets, and messages arrived.

2009 was also the year that the iPhone was refreshed without a radically new hardware design. This process of design evolution, instead of revolution, continues to this day with an "S" release every two years.

2010: iPhone 4

As the SpaceX Dragon Capsule returned to Earth on December 9th 2010, the world watched it happen live via a crystal clear video, thanks to the Retina Display on their new iPhone 4. This pin-sharp screen packed 326 pixels into every inch of the screen,

giving text the same sharpness as traditional printed text, and making images and video look richer and more lifelike than ever before. We now take ultra-sharp mobile screens for granted, but at the time it was revolutionary.

Other new features included with the iPhone 4 were its 5 megapixel camera that recorded 720p HD video; the A4 chip for improved graphics capability; and a front-facing camera for making FaceTime calls; and while the iPhone 4 was similar in size to its predecessor, it came with a stunning new design: an uninsulated stainless steel frame sandwiched between two plates of glass. Customers instantly fell in love with it, and by the end of 2010 47 million units had been sold.

2011: iPhone 4s

As Game of Thrones fans recovered from the shock of the first season's finale, the iPhone

4S was unleashed upon the world. As with the iPhone 3GS, the 4s looked remarkably similar in design to its predecessor, but alongside a re-designed antenna that improved signal strength, it also included the A5 chipset; an eight-megapixel camera with support for 1080p video recording; and iOS 5, which introduced iCloud, iMessage, Notification Center and Siri.

The press heaped praise on the new device. The Verge's Joshua Topolsky stated that "...if this were to be a car, it would be a Mercedes" and finished by saying "Is this the best phone ever made? That's debatable. But I can tell you this: the iPhone 4S is pretty damn cool."

2012: iPhone 5

This was the year that saw the Tesla Model S go into production; an electric vehicle that has upended the car industry, and is years ahead of the competition. In many ways, it's the iPhone of the automobile world.

The same year on September 12th, iPhone 5 was announced. It featured a brand new design with an aluminum-composite frame, it

was 18% thinner than the iPhone 4s, 20% lighter and had 12% less overall volume. Inside it featured the A6 chip, a 1.3GHz dual-core processor and 1GB of RAM. It debuted with iOS 6, which introduced an entirely new Maps app, the Passbook app, Siri enhancements and Facebook integration.

Pre-orders for the iPhone 5 went live on September 14th, 2012. Within 24 hours, more than two million orders had been received. When the device finally went on sale September 21st, the total number of pre-orders was more than 20 times of the iPhone 4s. Press reviews were favorable, with Tim Stevens from Engadget stating "This is a hallmark of design. This is the one you've been waiting for," and The Verge's Joshua Topolsky declaring "...for the mass market, it's the best smartphone, period."

2013: iPhone 5s & iPhone 5c

This was the year that twerking became a thing. Also, China landed a rover vehicle on the Moon. It was also the year that Apple launched two new iPhones: the iPhone 5S and the iPhone 5C.

The 5S retained the familiar look of the iPhone 5, with the only significant visual change being a new gold color option. Look a little closer, however, and there was one other subtle external change: the Touch ID fingerprint sensor. This new feature enabled the iPhone 5S to recognize fingerprints, allowing the device to be unlocked with a touch of a finger. Internally, the iPhone 5S featured the 64-bit A7 processor, which was twice as fast as the previous generation, and the rear camera included a new 5-element lens with a f/2.2 aperture that was 15% larger than before.

The iPhone 5C was just as interesting. It was the first iPhone since the 3G to come in an all-plastic enclosure, and it came in five colors: green, blue, yellow, pink, and white.

2014: iPhone 6

It seemed like the long-promised gaming revolution known as virtual reality was about to be realized in 2014, when the Oculus Rift developer kit unit became available to buy. It ushered in a new, immersive world of gaming that brought worlds to life like never before, but it was also buggy and plagued by a low-resolution screen. Thankfully, the iPhone 6 came with a pin-sharp Retina Display that was .7-inches larger than earlier models, while it's bigger brother, the iPhone 6 Plus, stunned the world with a massive 5.5-inch screen. The iPhone was finally growing up.

Alongside the larger displays, the iPhone 6 and 6 Plus featured a radical overhaul to its design. For the first time, the screen curved at the edges to seamlessly meet the metal surface that covered the back, making it more comfortable to hold. It was thinner than any iPhone to date, but packed more power and had a longer battery life.

Internally, the iPhone 6 had plenty of new features to offer. Its all-new barometer chip sensed the air pressure to work out your relative elevation. That meant it could now track how many flights of stairs you had climbed, or the height of the hill you were walking, ensuring fitness apps could accurately work out how many calories you had burned during the day. It's upgraded 8-megapixel camera was larger than ever, with 1.5-micron-sized pixels and a f/2.2 aperture, while the front-facing camera captured 81% more light and could take up to 10 photos a second. Both iPhone 6 and iPhone 6 Plus could now record 1080p high-definition video at 60 frames-per-second, making action shots look more lifelike and cinematic. Both iPhones featured better battery life than previous models, with 16 days of standby time, 80 hours of audio playback and 12 hours of 3G browsing. All these new features ensured iPhone 6 and iPhone 6 Plus were the best iPhones to date.

2018: iPhone 8

As the Tesla Model 3 went on sale to employees, iPhone 8 was announced at the Apple Keynote September Event, alongside iPhone X, which we'll get to in the next chapter.

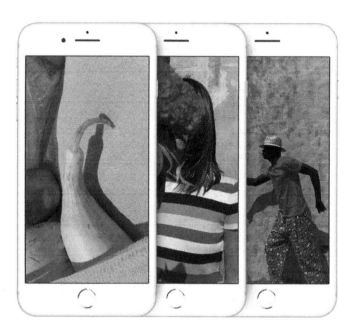

The iPhone 8 and 8 Plus might look similar to the iPhone 7, but every element of its hardware was been improved to make it a more beautiful and powerful device. Externally, the iPhone 8 came in three new glass finishes: space grey, silver, and gold. It had the most durable glass ever in a smartphone; glass that had been reinforced by a laser-welded, aerospace-grade aluminum band.

The display of iPhone 8 and 8 Plus introduced True Tone technology to adjust the white balance of the display to match the surrounding environment, making images look more natural and vibrant. It also had an expansive color spectrum to make content pop off the screen. To ensure music, calls and video sounded better than before, the iPhone 8 featured a redesigned stereo system that was 25% louder than the iPhone 7.

iPhone 8 continued to support Touch ID, enabling users to unlock the phone with just a fingertip. The use of the Home button for Touch ID ensured the device looked remarkably similar to previous devices, while keeping the same screen-to-device ratio. Other improvements included the A11 Bionic chip, dual 12MP cameras, and wireless charging, all of which are shared with the iPhone X; released alongside the iPhone 8.

2018: iPhone X

iPhone X was the biggest leap forward since the original iPhone, and promised to set the course for the next 10 years of smartphone development.

 Like the iPhone 8, it had glass on both the front and back of the device, with a stainless steel band that wrapped around the middle. It was water and dust resistant, and came in two finishes; space grey and silver. It also had an all-new display, called the Super Retina Display. At 5.8-inches in sizes and with a 2436x1125 resolution, it was the highest pixel density display ever shipped with an iPhone.

iPhone X was the first device from Apple to include an OLED screen that also supported HDR content. It also included True Tone technology ,which adjusted the white balance of the screen to match the ambiance around the device.

iPhone X was perhaps most recognizable by a small notch which ran along the top of the display. So recognizable was this notch that rival phone manufacturers quickly began to copy the design, releasing phones with the same notch, but with minor changes to avoid any copyright infringements. The notch on iPhone X housed some of the most sophisticated technology ever developed for an iPhone. Called the TrueDepth Camera System, it included an ambient light sensor, speaker, Proximity Sensor, Flood Illuminator, microphone, 7MP camera, infrared camera, and a dot projector; all of which worked in tandem to recognize your face, play audio, and enable you to make video calls.

Other new features exclusive to the iPhone X included new gestures to replace the Home button, a taller screen (12-13% additional screen area, when compared to earlier 4.7" iPhones), and cameras orientated vertically on the back, instead of horizontally.

iPhone XS and XS Max

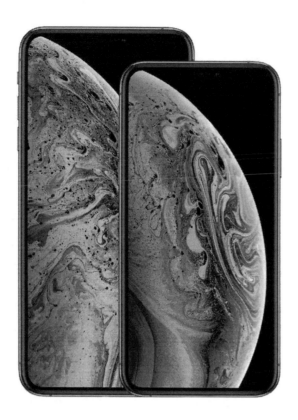

Every odd year, the iPhone receives an "S" update. Think of it as a spec bump. The design stays the same, but everything inside gets refreshed and upgraded with better specifications. In short, they get faster, the cameras get better, and the hardware is refined even more. 2018 was no different, as it sees the release of both the iPhone XS and the iPhone XS Max.

Before we go any further, it's worth noting that the iPhone XS is pronounced "iPhone ten s", not "iPhone excess". Same goes for the Max, it's "iPhone ten s max", not "iPhone excess max". It's an easy mistake to make.

A quick overview

With iPhone X, the entire device is the display. It has an all-new 5.8-inch Super Retina, with a 2436x1125 resolution. That's 458 pixels-per-inch, making it the highest pixel density display ever shipped with an iPhone.

As you might expect, the iPhone XS is the most advanced iPhone Apple has ever created. It's made form a surgical-grade stainless steel, it has a gorgeous new gold finish on the front and back, it has better cameras, and of course, there's a bigger version to choose from: the iPhone XS Max.

iPhone XS comes in three colors: gold, silver, and space grey. They're protected from dust and liquids to an IP68 rating. That means you can drop your iPhone into a liquid of two meters deep, for up to 30-minutes, and not see any damage to the internal components. That includes most types of liquid too. The iPhone XS has been tested in clean water, sea water, chlorinated water, tea, and even beer.

The screen on iPhone XS is a Super Retina display, which basically means it's super sharp, supports HDR content, and it simply looks incredible. If you watch the latest movies, such as LEGO Batman, then you'll get to enjoy them with both Dolby Vision and HD10 support; so colors look rich and lifelike, while light and shadow has an incredible depth to it. Similarly, any photos you take using the iPhone XS will look incredibly realistic when viewed back on its screen.

This year, the iPhone XS comes in two sizes: one with a 5.8-inch display, and another with a 6.5-inch display. This latter model (if you didn't already know), is called the iPhone XS Max, and it has the biggest display ever shipped on an iPhone. Here's a quick image comparing both iPhone XS and iPhone XS Max with the iPhone 8 Plus:

As you can see, the display on the iPhone XS Max dwarfs that on the previous iPhone 8 Plus. Similarly, the iPhone XS Max has a taller display, enabling you to see more content.

Design and Display

With both iPhone XS and the iPhone XS Max, the entire device is the display. The iPhone XS includes a 5.8-inch OLED Super Retina Display, with a 2436x1125 resolution. That's 458 pixels-per-inch, or 2.7 million pixels in total, making it incredibly dense and detailed. The iPhone XS Max goes even further. It has a 6.5-inch display, with a 2688x1242 resolution. That's 3.3 million pixels in total, and the same 458 pixels-per-inch density.

Both displays use complex hardware and manufacturing techniques to enable curved corners that closely follow the curves and contours of each device. Software built into iOS then uses subpixel anti-aliasing to ensure pixels towards the edge of the display are distortion-free.

A small notch along the top of the display houses some of the most sophisticated technology ever developed for an iPhone. Called the TrueDepth Camera System, it contains the following sensors and emitters to enable face recognition:

- Ambient light sensor
- Speaker
- Proximity Sensor
- Flood Illuminator
- Microphone
- 7MP camera
- Infrared Camera
- Dot Projector

The notch at the top of the display is always present. iOS doesn't attempt to hide the notch, but instead owns it, showing content on either side at all times. Usually, the time is shown to the left of the notch, with the cellular network, Wi-Fi, and battery to the right. These change color depending on the background and content shown beneath. When background tracking, a recording or a call is enabled, the time appears above a colored rectangle. When full-screen apps or games are being displayed, the notch is still present. When media is playing in landscape mode, such as a video, the notch appears but can be hidden by zooming the media content out.

Both iPhone XS and XS Max are dominated by their beautiful displays, but the rest of its hardware is just as interesting. On the back of iPhone XS is the most durable glass ever in an iPhone, ensuring drops and bangs don't smash or damage the casing. A seven-layer ink process enables the iPhone to come in three colors: Space Grey, Silver, or Gold; while an oleophobic coating helps to prevent smudges and fingerprints from sticking to the glass.

Wireless Charging

The glass back, together with an efficient charging system, allows iPhone XS to be charged using any wireless charger typically found in hotels, restaurants, airports, and cars. iPhone XS uses the open standard Qi to provide wireless charging, which is widely recognized and already supported; you can already buy wireless charging docks on the web - just look for the Qi logo.

Both iPhone XS and XS Max feature improved wireless charging when compared to the iPhone 8 and X. Typically, you can expect the XS to get to a full charge about 30-minutes faster than the X. Both XS and XS Max are also less sensitive to where you place the iPhone on the charger.

A12 Bionic

iPhone XS is powered by the A12 Bionic. It includes two performance cores, used for processor-intensive tasks such as gaming or editing photos, with a further four lower-powered cores for everyday tasks such as browsing the web. Overall, the A12 Bionic chip is 15% faster than the one found in the iPhone X, while using up to 50% less power. This means you'll get (on average), about 30-minutes more battery life per-day while using the iPhone XS, and up to one hour extra battery time using the iPhone XS Max.

Dual 12MP Cameras

Both iPhone XS and XS Max have two 12MP cameras on the back of the device, which are packed with the most advanced photography systems seen yet on an iPhone. Here's a full rundown of their complete specifications:

- Dual 12MP wide-angle and telephoto cameras
- Wide-angle: ƒ/1.8 aperture
- Telephoto: ƒ/2.4 aperture
- 2x optical zoom; digital zoom up to 10x
- Portrait mode with advanced bokeh and Depth Control
- Portrait Lighting with five effects (Natural, Studio, Contour, Stage, Stage Mono)
- Dual optical image stabilization

- Six-element lens
- Quad-LED True Tone flash with Slow Sync
- Panorama (up to 63MP)
- Sapphire crystal lens cover
- Backside illumination sensor
- Hybrid IR filter
- Autofocus with Focus Pixels
- Tap to focus with Focus Pixels
- Smart HDR for photos
(continued on next page)

19

these notifications appear on your device via the Settings app, but now, with iOS 12, you can also change these settings from the Lock screen. To do this, press firmly on a notification and a Manage panel will slide up from the bottom of the screen, with two large buttons: Deliver Quietly, and Turn Off…

Delivery Quietly
Press Deliver Quietly, and any further notifications from this source will only appear inside Notification Center, so you won't see any more Lock Screen notifications from this source, banners, app icon badges, or hear any sounds.

Turn Off
Press Turn Off, and you'll switch off all future notifications.

Screen Time
Ever wonder if you're spending too much time in Facebook? Do you ever think to yourself, "did I really spend the entire night watching YouTube videos?" Now you can find out exactly what you've been doing on your device, with the helpful Screen Time feature.

It's a new panel added to the Settings app, and not only does it provide details on app usage, but also the number of times you've picked up your phone during the day, how many notifications you've received, and how long the screen has been active. You can also set time limes for apps, or block inappropriate content. You'll find a detailed tutorial on this new feature in the Settings section of the book.

Do Not Disturb
Do Not Disturb During Bedtime
Have you ever woken up in the middle of the night, only to find yourself unable to fall back asleep again? It can be incredibly frustrating. Little triggers can set it off, like an unusual sound, a full bladder, or worse: a screen full of notifications on the bedside table. Now, with iOS 12, when Do Not Disturb kicks in overnight, you won't see any notifications appear on your device's screen. Instead, you'll see nothing but the time set against a black background. When the morning comes around, you'll see a welcome message and the weather; then, when you're ready to face

the day, all of your notifications will appear on-screen.

New Do Not Disturb options
With iOS 12, you can now set Do Not Disturb to end automatically in an hour, at the end of the day, when you leave a certain location, or at the end of a meeting on your calendar. Do this this, just press firmly on the Do Not Disturb icon within Control Center.

Augmented Reality (AR)

Gaming and AR-focused apps get even better in iOS 12, with added support for persistent experiences, facing tracking, and more...

Persistent and multiuser experiences
AR experiences can now be shared across time and fixed to actual locations. This means that if you create a piece of AR art, it can later be viewed in the same place by someone else.

3D object recognition
ARKit 2 recognizes objects and how your device is oriented to them. It can then use that information to trigger unique AR experiences.

Face tracking
Face tracking is now more accurate. I can see where you're looking, and detect whether you're sticking out your tongue or winking.

Scene reflection
Virtual AR objects can now reflect the real world in your camera.

USDZ file format
A new file format has been introduced which helps 3D creators to create rich content and animations optimized for mobile devices.

Measure app
A brand new app for both iPhone and iPad, Measure lets you automatically measure flat rectangular surfaces, and draw lines across flat surfaces to measure distances.

Photos

 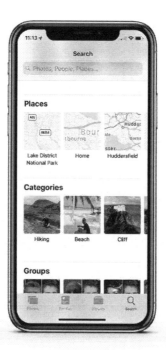 

The photos app sees a subtle re-design, with better search options, a new For You tab, plus more...

For You tab

A single destination for all of your Memories, Shared Album activity, and highlights in your library.

Sharing suggestions

The Photos app understands when you've done something meaningful, like taken a trip or attended an event, and will suggest sharing any photos you take with the people who are in them.

Intelligent search suggestions

As you search for events, people, places, and dates, the Photos app will make suggests before you finish typing.

Places search

You can search for photos based on the places or businesses where you were when you took them, whether it's a general category, like "Indian restaurant," or a specific place, like "IKEA."

Multiple keyword search

Now you can combine keywords in searches, like "hiking" and "vacation".

RAW photo support

You can import and manage RAW photos onto your iPhone.

Redesigned Albums tab

The Albums section has been completely revamped, with a horizontal layout for existing albums, and a list format for types of images.

FaceTime

Quite possibly the best way to make video calls on your iPhone or iPad, FaceTime has enabled millions of people to communicate with others around the world, for free. Now, with iOS 12, it has received a massive amount of new features and content...

Group FaceTime

FaceTime has been around for eight years, which probably makes it older than many of its users. Since its release back in 2010, FaceTime has done a pretty good job enabling two people to call and see each other, whether over video and audio, or just audio on its own. Now, with iOS 12, FaceTime finally supports group chats, with a total maximum number of 32 simultaneous callers.

Focus View in Group FaceTime

During a Group FaceTime call, whoever is speaking will automatically be front and center. Alternatively, you can double-tap the person you'd like to see.

Ringless notification

Group FaceTime uses a silent notification which participants can use to tap and join.

Messages integration

Group FaceTime calls can be initiated from a group Messages conversation. Active calls can also be joined from the conversation list, or within the conversation itself.

Animoji

While making a FaceTime call, you can now use Animoji or Memoji to replace your head. Sounds creepy, but it's a whole lot of fun.

Filters

While making a FaceTime call, you can transform your look using built-in filters such as black and white, and comic book.

Text effects

You can also add text effects like speech bubbles and emoji to your photos or videos.

Shapes

Or jazz up your photos and videos with shapes such as stars, hearts, and arrows.

iMessage sticker packs

Sticker packs can now be downloaded from the App Store for iMessage, to enhance your photos and videos. Stickers also track the movement of your face and move with you.

Private end-to-end encryption

FaceTime is fully encrypted for both one-to-one and group calls, so your conversations remain private and viewable only by the participants.

Updated Maps

Over the last four years, Apple has been working on improvements to the data and detail displayed within the Maps app, and with iOS 12, it's finally starting to show.

At the time of publication, only the areas around San Fransisco have been updated, but if you take a look you'll see more detail in ground cover, foliage, pools, pedestrian pathways and more. Maps will also become more responsive to changes as they happen, so road works and closures will appear quicker.

Performance

Faster and more responsive

iOS 12 has been overhauled for improved performance on devices as far back as the iPhone 5s and the iPad Air. Across the board, the things you do every day are faster than ever.

Smoother animations

Animations are smoother across the system, so when you do something like bring up Control Center, or multitasking between apps, everything is more fluid and responsive.

Up to 40% faster app launch

Your apps launch faster in day-to-day use. When you're multitasking between lots of apps, they also launch up to 2x faster.

Camera

Improved Portrait Lighting

Portrait mode photos are better than before. The Camera app can now generate a mask whenever it detects a person, and ten intelligently separate the person from the scene.

Portrait Segmentation API

A new API for third-party developers has been introduced, which allows for the separation of layers in a photo, such as separating the background from the foreground.

Improved QR code reader

The Camera can now highlight QR codes in the frame, making them easier to scan.

Up to 50% faster keyboard display

The keyboard appears 50% faster, while typing is more responsive.

Up to 70% faster swipe to Camera

Swiping to the Camera from the Lock Screen happens even faster, so you never miss a moment.

Up to 2x faster Share sheet display under load

The Share sheet loads up to twice as fast as it did in iOS 11, especially if you have a lot of sharing extensions installed.

Siri

Siri suggestions
A quicker way to do the things you do most often. As Siri learns your routines, you'll get suggested shortcuts for just what you need, at just the right time, on the Lock screen or in search.

Add to Siri
Add shortcuts to Siri to run them with your voice on your iPhone, iPad, Apple Watch, or HomePod.

New Shortcuts app
Create or customize your own shortcuts to run multiple steps at once. Get started with examples from the gallery and personalize with steps from across your apps.

Shortcuts API
App developers can work with Siri to run shortcuts via a new SiriKit API.

Motorsports
Get live standings, schedules, rosters, and stats.

Translation
Translate phrases into many more languages, with support for over 40 language pairs.

Celebrity facts
Check facts about celebrities, such as "What is Gillian Flynn's latest novel?" or "Where was Amy Adams born?"

Food knowledge
Ask Siri questions about food and get answers from the USDA database, including calories, vitamins, and how healthy a food is overall. For example, ask "How much caffeine in coffee?" or "How healthy is fish?"

iPhone XS Hardware

So you've unboxed your iPhone, and it's a stunning piece of hardware. Here's what all of it's buttons and ports do, and what you get included in the box.

iPhone Hardware

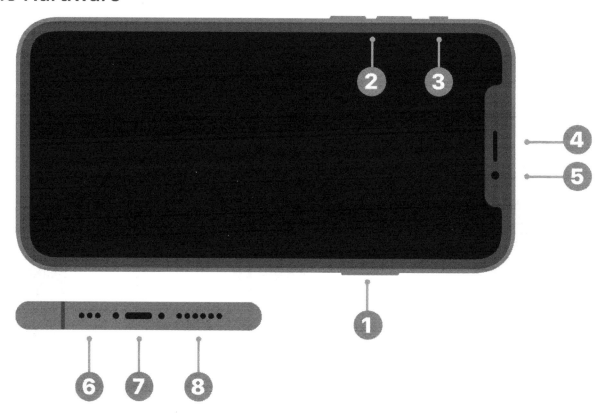

1. **Power/Side Button.** Press this to turn your iPhone on. You can also double press it to enable Apple Pay, or hold it down to activate Siri.

2. **Volume up/down.** Press these to alter the volume of audio on your iPhone, you can also use these to take a photo when using the Camera app.

3. **Ring/Silent.** Flip this switch to mute your iPhone.

4. Speaker/Microphone.

5. **Front-facing camera**. For the best selfies, look into this small lens when taking a photo.

6. **Microphone**. Try not to cover this up when making a call.

7. **Lightning Connector.** Plug your Lightning Cable into this port to charge your iPhone.

8. **Stereo Speaker.**

What's in the box

1. **EarPods.** They're actually pretty good, but they don't block outside noise. To use these simply plug them into the Lightning Connector on the bottom of your iPhone.

2. **iPhone XS.** Nothing more needs to be said.

3. **USB cable.** Use this cable to charge your iPhone via the...

4. **Power Adaptor**. Plus this straight into the wall.

5. **Documentation**. Not pictured here, but it looks like a small white pocketbook.

How to transfer data from your old iPhone to a new one

Getting a new iPhone is really exciting. Especially if your old one broke and you haven't been able to check your messages for a while. But transferring all your contacts, photos, apps, and other random stuff isn't so exciting. It's time consuming, technical, and quite simply a tedious chore. Thankfully, it's straightforward if you're going from one iPhone to another.

That's because most iPhone's automatically back up all their data on a daily basis. I say most because some people choose to turn this feature off for security reasons (trust me, you don't need to worry about backing up your iPhone to iCloud). For those who have turned off iCloud backups, then there's another way to transfer all your stuff from one iPhone to another. We'll get to it in a minute.

Before you begin...

If you have an Apple Watch, make sure to unpair it from your old iPhone before you set up the new one. To do this open the **Apple Watch** app, tap **My Watch**, select your watch, tap the **info** button then tap **Unpair Apple Watch**.

You can re-pair it to the new device during the setup process.

Use iCloud to set up your new iPhone

If you've been regularly backing up your iPhone to iCloud, then read on to learn how to copy all of your iCloud things to the new iPhone. If you're not sure, you can check and enable it by opening the **Settings** app, then **iCloud** > **Backup**.

1. Power on your new device. A "Hello" screen will appear.
2. Follow the steps to add a Wi-Fi network, then when you see the Apps & Data screen, tap **Restore from iCloud Backup**.
3. Sign into iCloud using your Apple ID and password.
4. Choose the most recent backup. You can check by looking at the date and size of each backup.
5. If you've purchased apps and iTunes content using multiple Apple IDs then you'll be asked for the passwords to each one.

6. Wait for the process to finish. This may take some time, so it's a good idea to keep your device connected to Wi-Fi and a power source.
7. After the process has completed your device will turn on and activate, but it will still need to download content such as apps and photos, so be patient as it restores all of your data.

Use Quick Start to transfer data

If you didn't use iCloud to back up your files, then using the Quick Start is just as easy. It lets you wirelessly copy all of your things from one iPhone to another, so long as both devices are within a few feet of each other. Here's how it works:

1. Begin by transferring your sim card from the old iPhone or iPad to the new one.
2. Turn on your new iPhone and place it next to your old one. The Quick Start screen will automatically appear, and offer the option of using your Apple ID to set up the new device. Make sure it's the right Apple ID, then tap **Continue**.
3. Wait for an animation to appear on your new device, then use the camera viewfinder on the old device and center the animation in the middle of the screen. When you see a button that says **Finish on New [Device]**, tap the button and follow the on-screen options to transfer your apps, data, and settings to the new device.
4. If you have an Apple Watch, you'll be asked if you would like to transfer your Apple Watch data and settings too.

Face ID

One of the most sci-fi features of the iPhone is its ability to instantly scan your face with a dot projector, then automatically unlock it or let you buy things. It's a feature called Face ID, and it's way more advanced than you might think.

It works by using a TrueDepth Camera System to recognize you. Basically, an infrared camera can see your face, even in the dark, while a dot projector maps your face with more than 30,000 dots. All of this data is used to create a mathematical model of your face. This mathematical model is used to prevent people from using photos of your to unlock your iPhone. The Face ID also looks for telltale signs of life (like moving or blinking eyes), to know that a model of your face wasn't used. Once it has confirmed all of this (which usually takes less than a second) then Face ID tells your iPhone that it's definitely you; and that things are good to go.

Here's a nice little fact: when using Face ID, there's a 1 in a million chance that someone else can unlock your device by looking at it.

How to set up Face ID

1. Your iPhone will ask you to setup Face ID when you activate it for the very first time. If you skipped that step, just open the **Settings** app, select **Face ID & Passcode** then tap **Enrol Face**.
2. Follow the on-screen instructions to add your face. You'll be asked to gently move your face in a circular motion. Face ID performs best when all angles of your face are captured.
3. Once the process is complete, tap **Continue** to enrol your face.

To unlock your iPhone using Face ID, toggle **iPhone Unlock** on. Next time you lift your iPhone off the table, or tap the screen, it will automatically scan your face and unlock.

To use Face ID for making purchases, toggle **iTunes & App Store** on. Now, when you purchase an app, movie or TV show, tap the price icon to purchase it, your face will be automatically scanned and the download will begin.

To automatically use Face ID to log you into websites, toggle **Safari Autofill** on. When you're next asked to enter your name and password, your face will be scanned automatically and your details will be entered into the website.

How to quickly disable Face ID

If you're worried that someone might want to coerce you into unlocking your iPhone X with your face, just press the power button five times and it will enter Emergency SOS mode. This disables Face ID, meaning you can only unlock your iPhone using your six-digit passcode.

Set up an alternative look

If you sometimes change your look in a drastic way (for example via makeup, with a wig, or with extensive accessories), then you can teach Face ID to recognize you with these changes. To do this, get ready with your alternative look, then go to **Settings** > **Face ID & Passcode**, then tap **Set Up an Alternate Appearance**. You can now re-scan your face, and your iPhone will recognize it in the future.

The Lock Screen

Lift up your iPhone and (so long as it's turned on) the Lock Screen will quickly fade into view. If you've received any notifications, such as a text message or a news story, then you'll see them in the middle of the screen. Otherwise, you'll just see the background wallpaper, time, and date.

If your iPhone is on a desk and you don't want to pick it up, then you can also tap on the screen to display the Lock Screen.

Unlock your iPhone XS

To unlock your iPhone XS, simply look at the screen. When you see the padlock icon unlock, then the device has been unlocked using Face ID.

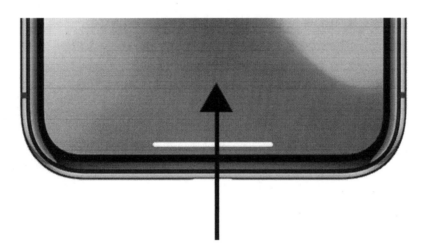

If you've just restarted, activated Emergency SOS mode, or if your face cannot be recognized, you'll need to enter your passcode to unlock your iPhone.

Access Control Center

Swipe down from the top-right corner and you'll open Control Center. From here you can adjust settings, toggle features and even control Apple TV. If you're using an iPhone with a Home button, then swipe up from the bottom of the screen to access Control Center.

Access Spotlight

While viewing the Lock Screen, swipe down from the top-left corner and you'll access Spotlight, where all your widgets, shortcuts and Spotlight search can be found. If you're using an iPhone with a Home button, then swipe down from the middle of the screen to access Control Center.

See any notifications

Place your finger in the middle of the Lock screen then slide upwards to see all of your notifications. You can clear groups of notifications by tapping the small X button. If you press firmly then you'll see an option to clear all your notifications at once.

Interact with notifications

If a message arrives you can tap the notification bubble to send a reply without even unlocking your device. This method of interaction works with other notifications too including Wallet passes and third-party apps.

Take a photo

From the Lock Screen, tap the Camera button or swipe to the right and you'll instantly open the Camera app. It's possible to take a photo, capture video or record time-lapse footage, and you can immediately view anything you take by tapping the thumbnail button in the bottom-left corner of the screen. It's worth noting, however, that you can't access the rest of your photo library without unlocking the device first.

Activate the Flashlight

See the torch icon on the lower-left side of the screen? Tap it and you'll activate the LED flashlight on the back of your iPhone. This acts as a great flashlight in dark areas.

The Home Screen

The Home screen is the first port of call for nearly everything you do on iPhone. From here you can open and organize apps, get instant feedback on battery life and see the time and network status. You can get back to the Home screen at any time by swiping up from the bottom of the screen.

Take a look at the top of the screen and you'll see a selection of status icons alongside each side of the cut-out notch. These help you to instantly recognize if the battery is low, if any data-aware apps are running in the background, if an app is recording audio, or most obvious of all: what time it is. Let's take a look at what each icon means:

Time

Glance at this set of numbers to see what time it is. You can toggle it between 12 and 24-hour time by opening the **Settings** app and going to **General** > **Date & Time** > **24-Hour Time**.

Signal Strength

These five vertical lines represents the signal strength of your carrier, so the more filled-in circles you see, the stronger the signal. Look to the right of the signal strength icons and you'll see the name of your data carrier.

Wi-Fi

This icon appears when you're connected to a Wi-Fi network. Just like the signal strength icons, the more filled in the icon is, the stronger the connection.

Battery

This icon and percentage count displays how much battery life remains. You can toggle the percentage count on and off by going to **Settings** > **Battery** > **Battery Percentage**.

Headphones

This icon appears when a pair of Bluetooth headphones are connected with your iPhone.

Airplane mode

Turn Airplane mode on via Control Center or the Settings app and you'll see this icon.

Location Data

This icon appears when an app is tracking your location. For example, you might be using the Maps app, or perhaps a fitness app that monitors your distance and speed.

Notifications

This small red icon appears when an app has a notification for you, such as a new email or message. You will also see it above the Settings app when a Software Update is available.

Delete an app

If you've downloaded an app but want to remove it, simply tap and hold on the app icon, then tap

the cross key that appears when the app starts to wiggle.

Move apps

To rearrange an app on the home screen of your device, tap and hold on its icon, then slide the app to wherever you wish to place it. When you're finished, tap the Done button in the top-right corner.

Create a folder for apps

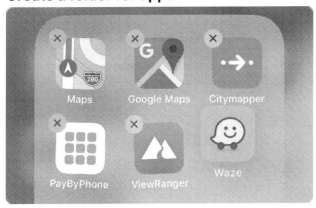

You can arrange apps within folders to better organize your home screen. To do this, simply tap and hold on an app, then drag it on top of another app. A folder will be created and named automatically, but you can rename the folder by tapping on the name and entering your own via the keyboard.

Gestures and Buttons

The vast, high-definition screen that spreads out across your iPhone is a technological marvel. You might not know it, but it actually supports up to 10 individual fingertips, and works by detecting the static charge on your skin — not heat or pressure as many often believe. By tapping and gesturing on the screen you can take full advantage of everything iOS has to offer, such as zooming into content, rotating images and more.

Additionally, the hardware buttons on your device enable you to mute the device, enable Apple Pay, enable Siri or shut the entire thing off. Many of these functions are entirely intuitive, but for those who have never interacted with an iPhone before, let's go over them...

Return to the Home screen
Whenever you're in an app, swipe up from the very bottom of the screen to return to the Home screen.

Access the multitasking screen
Swipe up from the bottom of the screen then stop halfway to see all the apps you've recently opened. Once there, you'll see a large thumbnail of all your recently opened apps. Tap on one to go back to it, or scroll through the apps to see more.

Jump between apps
Want to quickly jump between apps? Just swipe along the very bottom of the screen, left-to-right, and you'll jump between apps.

Access Search
From the Home screen, pull the screen down using your finger to access the Search screen appear. From here you can search for apps, emails, contacts and more. You'll also see app and web search suggestions based on your history and recent activity.
app.

Swipe to go back
Want to go back a panel or page? Just swipe from the left-side of the screen inwards and you'll go back to the previous area. This works great for going back a page in Safari, or for going back to your Mailboxes in the Mail

Access Siri
To talk to Siri - your personal voice-activated assistant - just press and hold the Power button on the side of your iPhone Xs. You can also say "Hey Siri" out-loud to enable Siri.

Access Apple Pay

To quickly pull up your debit and credit cards, double-press the Power button on the side of your iPhone Xs.

Control the volume

See those two large buttons on the left side of your iPhone? They control the volume levels. Tap each one to make music or ringtones sound louder or quieter. Additionally, hold down the lower volume button to quickly mute the device.

Power off your device

If you'd like to fully turn off your iPhone, then hold down both the power button and volume up button to turn off the device. After a few seconds, it will turn off. Press and hold this button again to turn iPhone back on.

Connect to a Wi-Fi Network

Connecting to a Wi-Fi network is one of those fundamental tasks that we all must do from time to time. Perhaps you're visiting a friend and would like to hook up to their internet connection, or you might be sat in a coffee shop that offers free Wi-Fi. Here's how to do it:

1. Open the **Settings** app then tap the **Wi-Fi** button.
2. If Wi-Fi isn't already turned on then tap the toggle button near the top of the screen.
3. Select a wireless network, and enter its password if necessary.
4. Tap the blue **Join** button on the keyboard. If you've entered the password successfully your device will automatically join the network.

Public networks

If the network doesn't require a password, then you can just tap on the Wi-Fi network name and immediately connect. Note, however, that sometimes networks require you to enter personal details via the Safari app before you can freely browse the web. You'll probably come across this situation in coffee shops and airports. Hotels might also request you to enter your hotel room number and a password, the latter of which is typically available from the reception.

Share a WiFi password between iOS devices

Looking for the WiFi password is always a pain. It's usually hidden on the back of a router, printed on an obscure piece of card or written in small print on a receipt. Over time this becomes less of a problem, as WiFi passwords are stored in your iCloud account, so once you connect to a network all of your devices will automatically join when they come within reach; but nevertheless, those new networks will still appear every now and then.

With iOS 12, joining WiFi networks becomes slightly easier, because you can automatically copy WiFi passwords from one iOS device to another. Here's how it works:

1. Enter the range of a new WiFi network
2. Place your iPhone near an unlocked iOS device that's already connected to the WiFi network
3. Your device will automatically ask the other device for the WiFi password
4. If the owner of the other device agrees to the request, you'll receive the password automatically and instantly connect.

How to use Control Center

Tucked above the screen are a helpful set of shortcut buttons for toggling common switches and settings. They include a slider for controlling screen brightness, a button for enabling Wi-Fi, shortcuts to toggle Airplane Mode, night Shift mode and more. To access these shortcuts at any time swipe down from the top-right corner of the screen. In an instant, you'll see Control Center appear as an overlay above the screen.

All of the toggles and buttons in Control Center support 3D Touch to show you further settings or more extensive controls. To use 3D Touch on a button just press firmly and it will expand beneath your finger.

To close Control Center swipe back up or tap in the empty space below Control Center.

Network and connection settings

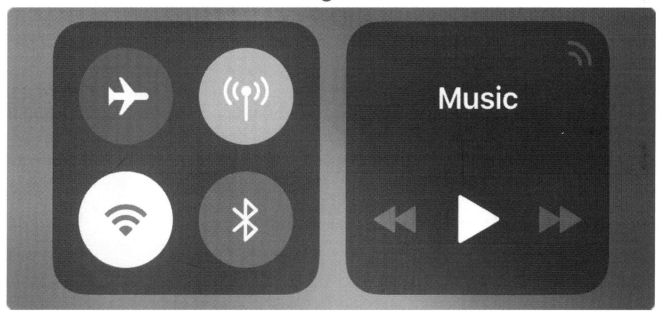

The rounded box in the top left corner of the screen is where you can access all the wireless and network settings for your device. By default, you'll see four controls for activating or disabling Airplane mode, your cellular connection, Wi-Fi and Bluetooth.

By pressing firmly on this box, you can also access controls for AirDrop and Personal Hotspot.

Music controls

The box in the upper right portion of the screen lets you control music playback and settings. By default you'll see the track name, play and fast-forward/skip. In the top-right corner of the box is a small icon (it looks like two curved lines) for choosing the playback device.

By pressing firmly on the music controls box you can expand it to show album artwork, a volume slider, and a timeline scrubber.

Orientation Lock

If you don't want the screen to rotate into landscape/portrait mode when you rotate the device, tap the Orientation Lock button.

Do Not Disturb

Tap the moon icon to turn on Do Not Disturb. While it's on you won't be bothered by phone calls, texts or any notifications, your device won't emit any noise and the screen won't turn on.

Press firmly on this device, and you'll be able to access various shortcuts to enable Do Not Disturb for a period of time, or until you leave a location.

Brightness and volume sliders

To the middle-right of Control Center are sliders for adjusting the device brightness and volume. Drag these sliders to change the screen brightness or volume, or press firmly to access larger controls that are easier to use.

Flashlight

Tap the Torch icon to instantly turn on the flash at the back of your iPhone. You can also press firmly to choose between bright, medium and low settings.

App shortcuts

Tap the Timer, Calculator or Camera button to instantly open these apps. You can also press firmly to activate features such as the flashlight brightness, timer length and video recording.

Customize Control Center

If you want to add additional buttons to Control Center, or remove those that you don't use very often, simply open the **Settings** app and tap **Control Center.** On the following panel you'll find shortcuts to add and remove options. You can also rearrange the options by using the drag buttons to customize Control Center to your exact needs.

Display Settings

The display of your iPhone is its most crucial component because it's the one you spend the most time prodding, poking, and stroking. Without a screen, the iPhone wouldn't be much better than one of those old rotary-dial phones. Just smaller, and with Siri.

You might not know it, but there are some essential settings available for the iPhone which let you adjust the screen to suit your needs better. You can play around with the brightness, enable True Tone, and capture what's on the screen to share with others...

Adjust the brightness

If you'd like to adjust the brightness of the display, just swipe down from the top-right corner of the screen to access Control Center, then slide the brightness slider up or down. You can also press firmly on the slider to enable a larger version that's easier to control.

Auto-Brightness

By default your device will automatically adjust the brightness of the display to match the conditions of your environment; so if you're in a dark room, the screen will dim, while under direct sunlight it will set to maximum brightness.

To turn this off or on, go to **Settings** > **General** > **Accessibility** > **Display Accommodations** and turn **Auto-Brightness** off.

Disable True Tone

True Tone is a brilliant feature that adjusts the screen ambience to match the environment around you. So if you're sitting in a room with yellowish light, the screen will subtly change to suit the environment.

If you're a designer and need more accurate color, or simply prefer the screen to always look pure white, open the **Settings** app and go to **Display & Brightness** and toggle **True Tone** off.

Alternatively, you can toggle True Tone off from Control Center. Just press firmly on the **brightness** slider, then tap the **True Tone** button which appears.

Change the text size

If your eyesight isn't perfect, then you might struggle to read small text on your iPhone's screen. Thankfully there's a slider switch that automatically increases - or decreases the text size on the user interface. To access this slider, go to **Settings** > **Display & Brightness**, then tap the **Text Size** option. On the following panel you'll be able to change text size by dragging the slider button.

Take a screenshot

If you want to share something interesting on your screen then taking a screenshot of it is a great way to do this. Here's how it works:

1. Press the **Power button** and **Volume Up** buttons at the same time to capture the screen.
2. You'll see a thumbnail of the screenshot minimize and snap to the bottom left corner.
3. Leave the thumbnail alone for a few seconds and it will disappear and save the screenshot to the Photos app. You can also swipe the thumbnail to the left to quickly save it.
4. Tap on the thumbnail and you can annotate it or delete it.
5. Press firmly on the thumbnail to quickly share it with others.

Create a video recording of the screen

If you need to capture your device's screen, then there's no need to use a third-party app, or Quicktime on a Mac. You can do it all using Control Center. Here's how:

1. Start by adding Screen Recording widget to Control Center. To do this go to **Settings** > **Control Center** > **Customize Controls** then add **Screen Recording**.
2. Close the Settings app and swipe up the screen to enable Control Center.
3. Tap the **Screen Recording** button (it looks like the outline of a circle with a dot in the middle) and after three seconds the recording will begin.
4. Tap the red bar at the top of the screen to stop the recording. It will then be added to Photos, where you can replay, edit or delete it.
5. To capture audio from your device's microphone, press firmly on the **Screen Recording** button within Control Center, then tap **Microphone Audio**.

Spotlight

 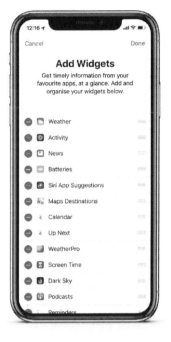 

You might not know it, but your iPhone knows a lot about your daily schedule and lifestyle. It's continually monitoring your calendar schedule, physical activity, messages, commute and more. Don't worry, this data isn't used for nefarious reasons; instead, it's used by the operating system to help you get home on time, achieve your fitness goals, meet all your appointments and more; all via the Spotlight screen.

How to access Spotlight

There are three ways to access the Spotlight screen:

1. Just raise your device or press the power/home button and any new spotlight information will appear on the Lock Screen. These might include new messages, map directions or your next calendar appointment.
2. From the Home screen, swipe to the right and Spotlight will appear.
3. If you're already within an app, you can access Spotlight by swiping down from the top-left corner to see Spotlight.

Spotlight Widgets

Spotlight widgets are small windows that display helpful information in a concise way. You might see the latest news stories, app suggestions, steps walked during the day or unread emails. Some widgets can be expanded to show more detail. You'll know because there will be a **Show More** button in the top-right corner of the widget. Tap this button and the widget will expand to reveal more information. Tapping **Show Less** will shrink the widget back to its original size.

Edit Spotlight Widgets

The entire Spotlight screen is customizable, and easily so. Simply swipe down to the bottom of the Spotlight screen then tap the **Edit** button. On the following screen you can delete and reorder widgets to best suit your needs. You can also add further widgets by scrolling down to the More Widgets section.

Interact with a notification widget

Whenever a notification arrives at the top of the screen – such as a new message – try dragging it downwards. You'll see the widget expand to almost fill the screen, letting you see more information and interact with content without ever actually opening an app.

Clear notifications

You can clear any notifications from Spotlight by swiping them to the left or by tapping the **X** button.

Prevent widgets from appearing on the Lock Screen

You can disable widgets on the Lock Screen at any time to prevent others from seeing your private information. To do this open the **Settings** app and go to **Touch ID & Passcode** > **Allow access when locked**.

Search using Spotlight

A helpful search bar at the top of the Spotlight screen lets you search for nearly anything. It's possible to search for apps, emails, messages, contacts, the weather, locations, businesses, news stories, the web and more.

Notifications

Whenever you receive a notification from a friend, app, or news source, you'll see a notification arrive in one of three ways:

1. If your device is locked, then the notification appears as a bubble on the Lock Screen.
2. If you're using your device when the notification arrives, then it will appear as a floating panel at the top of the screen.
3. If an app wants to get your attention, then you might see a red dot above its icon on the Home screen.

If you don't dismiss these notifications, then they will be saved in the Notification Center, which you can access by swiping down from the top of the screen.

Change how notifications appear on your device

To change an alert style for a notification, go to **Settings** > **Notifications** then select an app. Here are some of the alert styles you can choose from:

- **Allow Notifications:** Toggle on to receive notifications from the app you selected.
- **Sounds**: Toggle sound alerts for when you receive a notification.
- **Show on Lock Screen:** Turn on to see notifications on your Lock screen.
- **Show in History:** See previous notifications from the app you selected.

- **Banners:** Choose how you want notifications to appear when your device is unlocked. Tap Temporary to display alerts for a short period of time, or tap Persistent to have alerts stay on the screen until you act on it.
- **Show Previews:** Choose what you want to see when you get a notification, like a text message.

Clear all your notifications at once

If you have a stack of notifications waiting for you in Notification Center, then you can clear them all at once by pressing firmly on the small **X** button:

Reply to a message without using the Messages app

If a notification appears while you're using your device, pull it down from the top of the screen using your finger to interact with it. For example, if you get a message, pull the notification down and you'll be able to send a reply without going into the Messages app.

Grouped Notifications

When you receive multiple notifications from the same source (say, 10 messages from a friend), then these will appear as a "stack" of notifications on the Lock Screen. By tapping on this stack, you can expand it to see all of the earlier messages. You can also swipe across a group of notifications to manage them, view them or clear them all away.

Configure notifications from the Lock Screen

If you receive a notification from an app you don't want to hear from, then you can customize how any further notifications from this source will appear. To do this, press firmly on a notification, tap the options button (it looks like three dots) and a Manage panel will slide up from the bottom of the screen, with two large buttons: Deliver Quietly, and Turn Off...

Delivery Quietly

Press Deliver Quietly, and any further notifications from this source will only appear inside Notification Center, so you won't see any more Lock Screen notifications from this source, banners, app icon badges, or hear any sounds.

Turn Off

Press Turn Off, and you'll switch off all future notifications.

If you want to adjust notifications with more detail, then there's a **Settings** button at the bottom of the panel.

See where your friends are from Notification Center

Being able to track the location of your friends is a brilliant feature of the Find My Friends app, but it's also possible to quickly see the rough location of friends and their distance from your current location via the Notification Center panel. Here's how it works:

Start by opening Notification Center by swiping down from the top of the screen, then tap **Edit** at the bottom of the panel. Add the **Find Friends** widget by tapping the green plus button then tap **Done** to confirm.

Any friends that you're following will now appear with their thumbnail image and location, along with a helpful indicator of their distance from your current location.

Siri

Siri is your very own personal assistant. He (or she depending on your country of origin) can make calls for you, dictate emails and messages, make a restaurant reservation, remind you to do things, tell you about movies, make jokes and much more. Siri isn't perfect, however. It can't remember interactions from the past, it relies on hearing your voice in a clear manner, and it needs a connection to the internet to work. If you're aware of these limitations and don't mind the odd false request, then Siri can save time and even be a little fun to use.

Enable Siri

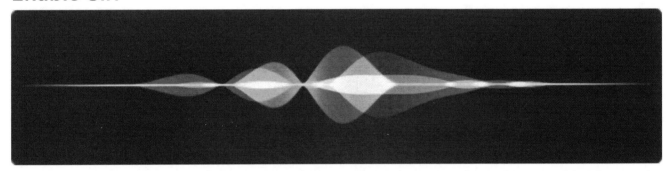

To enable Siri just hold down on the **Power** button. After two seconds you'll hear Siri chime and a small window will appear on the screen displaying a microphone. If using Siri for the first time then you'll see some tips suggestions. Tap the microphone icon. Siri is now listening for your voice.

Speak

Next, say out loud, "*What's the weather like today?*" Siri will automatically look for a weather report then tell you what it's going to be like. It's that simple to use Siri. When you're finished with Siri, press the **Power** button again, or swipe upwards.

Dictate text with Siri

If you'd like Siri to dictate a message or email, then simply say something like, "Tell Toby I'll be late". Siri will automatically create a new message or email to the recipient that says 'I'll be late home tonight'.

Dictate while writing a message

If you're already in the Messages or Mail app and would like Siri to dictate, simply tap the Microphone button on the keyboard next to the space key. Next, speak aloud the text you'd like Siri to dictate. As soon as you finish Siri will process the audio and add the text to the message or mail.

Activate Siri via voice command

It's possible to activate Siri by simply saying *"Hey Siri."* After you hear the recognizable Siri chime, say a command out loud (such as "tell me the time") and Siri will respond – all without your touch. To enable this feature, go to Settings > Siri & Search, and turn on Allow "Hey Siri".

Type to Siri

It's not always possible to talk out loud to Siri. In these cases you can type instead. To activate this feature go to **Settings** > **General** > **Accessibility** > **Siri**, then toggle **Type to Siri** on. Next time you activate Siri you'll see a keyboard fill the lower half of the screen, enabling you to type to Siri.

Use Siri Shortcuts

Added to iOS 12, Siri Shortcuts enable you to perform complicated actions with just a simple Siri command. For example, you can open your favourite website with a single word, or check for your favorite stock by just saying its name to Siri. Here's how it works:

1. Open the **Settings** app, then tap **Siri & Search**.
2. Select a suggested shortcut, or tap **More Shortcuts** to see more.
3. Record a personalized phrase.
4. Launch your shortcut by repeating that phrase to Siri.

Identify a song

If you'd like to find out what song is playing in the background just activate Siri and he/she will automatically begin listening to it. After a few seconds (depending on your signal strength) Siri will display details about the song and offer you the ability to play it via Apple Music.

Translate text

Siri is able to translate a phrase and speak it back to you in six languages: Mandarin Chinese, French, German, Italian and Spanish. At the time of publication it only works when Siri is set to US English. To translate text simply say out loud "*Hey Siri, how do I say it's nice to meet you in French?*" Siri will return the answer in both written and text format.

See what planes are overhead

Wondering where that distant plane is heading? To find out, activate Siri then say "*what flights are above me?*" or "*planes overhead*" and Siri will display a chart featuring the plane's flight airline, number, altitude and angle. Note that this feature is currently limited to the US, and it might take time to load depending on your signal strength.

Things to ask Siri:

There are countless questions you can ask Siri, but here are just a few examples of the wide-ranging topics and conversations you can have:

Video call via FaceTime:
"FaceTime Tom"

Play a music track:
"Play something by Monsters and Men"

Send a Message:
"Tell Dave I'll be right there."
or
"Send a message to Dave"

Calendar:
"Set up a meeting with Sarah at 9."

Maps:
"How do I get to Tom's?"
or
"Take me home."

Create a Reminder:
"Remind me to call Michael at 7."

Find a password:
"Show me my password for apple.com"

Mail:
"Email Chris to say I'm running late."

or
"Do I need to wear a rain coat?"

Weather:
"What's the weather for today?"

Stocks:
"What is the Microsoft stock price?"

Clock:
"Wake me up tomorrow at 10 a.m."
or
"Set a timer for 10 minutes"

Contacts:
"What's the address for Tim?"

Notes:
"Note that I spent $25 on shopping."
or
"Search for notes on budget."

WolframAlpha:
"How tall is the Statue of Liberty compared to the Empire State Building?"

Find friends:
"Find Toby"

Find your iPhone or iPad:
"Find my iPhone"

Post to Twitter:
"Tweet Siri is amazing"

Post to Facebook:
"Post to Facebook I'm having a great time today". This will show a Facebook post that reads "I'm having a great time today".

Movies:
"Show me movies directed by Steven Spielberg"
or
"I'd like to see a movie"

Sports:
"What's the score for the Giants game?"

iCloud

iCloud enables you to sync all of your images, videos, music, apps, contacts, calendars and much more across your iPhone and Mac or PC.

What does that mean? It means you can snap a photo on your iPhone then see it automatically appear on your Mac, PC, or Television. It means you can purchase a song, movie or TV show in iTunes and see it appear on all of your devices. It means you can start writing a document on your Mac, edit it on your iPhone and see the changes appear across both devices. You can also backup your device wirelessly, see where your friends are on a map, sync bookmarks and much more.

Photos

Any photo taken on your iPad or iPhone is wirelessly uploaded to iCloud, then automatically downloaded onto your other devices, Mac and/or PC. So you can take a photo during the day on your iPhone, then get home and view it larger on your Mac, all without having to sync or use wires.

iCloud Drive

iCloud Drive automatically saves all your documents created in Pages, Keynote, Numbers and Notes, then wirelessly beams them to your other devices. So if you're writing a letter or creating a presentation on your Mac, you'll be able to continue editing it on your iPad or iPhone without having to worry about saving it or transferring the file. Edits are automatically updated across all of your devices. It works like magic.

To access all the files in your iCloud Drive, simply open the **Files** app then select **iCloud Drive**.

Calendar, Contacts and Mail

Using iCloud, all of your emails, calendar entries and contacts are automatically synced across every iPhone and Mac. So if you update a phone number on your iPhone, the new number will automatically appear on your iPhone and Mac.

Safari

iCloud automatically saves your bookmarks, Reading Lists and open tabs. So if you're reading a lengthy web article on your Mac but need to dash, you can continue reading it at a later time on your iPad or iPhone. Simply tap on the iCloud bookmarks icon to see open tabs, or tap on the Bookmarks button to see all of your Bookmarks and Reading Lists.

Backup

iCloud automatically backs up your iPhone when it's plugged into a power source and connected to the web over Wi-Fi. iCloud backs up the following things: music, movies, TV shows, apps, books, photos and videos in the Camera Roll, device settings, app data, ringtones, app organization and messages. And if you buy a new iPhone, you can restore all of the above by using an existing iCloud backup.

Find My iPhone

If you can't find your iPhone, Find My iPhone will enable you to track it through iCloud. By signing into your iCloud account, either from www.icloud.com or another iPhone, you can see your devices on a map, set a passcode lock, remotely wipe them or send a message to the screen. You can also enable Lost Mode, whereby the device is automatically locked, a message with a contact appears on the screen and the device automatically tracks where it's been and reports it back to Find My iPhone.

Handoff

Handoff works by enabling you to start a task on your iPhone, then continue it on your Mac or iPad, or vice versa.

Take writing an email for example, you might begin to compose a message on your iPhone, then sit down at your desk and finish the email on your Mac. Maybe you're reading a web page on your iPhone, if you need a bigger screen you only need to turn on your iPad then swipe up to continue reading the page on the larger screen. Handoff is a simple and productive process that makes life so much easier. Here's how it works:

Requirements

Handoff requires a Mac running Yosemite or later to talk to your iPhone, so you'll need a 2012 iMac, MacBook Air, MacBook Pro, iMac or late 2013 Mac Pro. Additionally, you'll need to have Bluetooth enabled on every device, and they all need to be approximately 30 feet or less from each other.

Turn Handoff on

To enable Handoff on your iPhone, go to **Settings** > **General** > **Handoff & Suggested Apps**, then toggle the **Handoff** switch on. On the Mac, open **System Preferences**, click **General**, then ensure **Allow Handoff between this Mac and your iCloud devices** is ticked.

Jumping from iPhone to Mac

It's easy to swap tasks between an iPhone and Mac. Take reading a web page for example. When you open a web page on your iPhone, a Safari icon will appear on the left-side of the Dock on the Mac. Just tap on this icon to open the same webpage on your Mac. This same process goes for composing Notes, Emails and Messages, or adding Calendar and Contact entries.

Jump from iPhone to iPad

If you'd like to continue a task on your iPad, begin writing, adding or reading content on your iPhone, then turn on your iPad. On the Lock Screen you'll see the relevant app icon in the bottom left corner of the screen. Just tap or swipe it upwards to jump to the same content on your iPad. If the icon doesn't appear, ensure Bluetooth is turned on by swiping upwards to reveal Control Center, then tap the Bluetooth icon.

Apple Pay

Apple Pay is remarkable. You can use it to pay for items at the checkout with your iPhone, send money to friends, pay for tube or bus tickets, or buy items online without entering your credit card details. The experience is even better if you have an Apple Watch, because when you're ready to pay for something you only need to wave your wrist near the payment reader.

What is Apple Pay?

It's a way of paying for things by holding your iPhone or Apple Watch near a contactless payment terminal. You can also use it online to pay for goods without your credit card, or within apps when you see the Apple Pay logo, which looks like this:

  Buy with Pay   Pay

How to enable Apple Pay on your iPhone

The first step is to add a credit or debit card to the Wallet app, of which you can hold a maximum of eight. Here's how:

1. Open the **Wallet** app and follow the steps to add a card. If you're asked to enter the same card used with your iTunes account, you only need to enter its security code.
2. Tap **Next** and your bank will authorize and add your card. If your bank needs more details you can add these later via **Settings** > **Wallet & Apple Pay**, then tap on your new card.

How to use Apple Pay

It's surprisingly simple. When you're ready to pay for something, just hold your iPhone near the contactless reader, then when the screen turns on look at it to use Face ID to confirm the purchase.

You can also activate Apple Pay before making the purchase by pressing the **Power** button twice.

If you're using Safari and see the Apple Pay button at the checkout, just tap the button to make the purchase immediately.

If you're using an app and see the Apple Pay logo, you might need to toggle a setting that enables Apple Pay first — the app will let you know. Once enabled, tap the Apple Pay button, ensure all the details are correct, then place your finger on the Touch ID button to confirm the purchase.

Choose which card to use

The card linked to your Apple ID will automatically be the default card for Apple Pay, but you can change the default card via **Settings** > **Wallet & Apple Pay**.

If you don't want to change the default card then you can swap between them before making a purchase. To do this hold your iPhone near the contactless reader without resting your finger on the Touch ID sensor. When the screen turns on you will see the default payment card. Tap on it and you will be able to choose another.

See your recent transactions

Every time you use Apple Pay the last few transactions will be stored as virtual receipts on your iPhone. To see these open the **Settings** app, select **Wallet & Apple Pay**, tap on the credit/debit card of choice and any payments will appear in the **Transactions** section.

How to remove a debit or credit card

Open the wallet app, tap on the card you wish to remove them tap the **Info** icon that appears at the bottom of the screen. On the following panel you can remove the card by swiping to the bottom of the screen and tapping **Remove Card**.

Send or receive payments via Messages

Using Apple Pay it's possible to send or request money from anyone in your Contacts app using the Messages app. It's surprisingly easy and intuitive, and makes online transactions a whole lot easier. Please note, however, that Apple Pay within Messages isn't available in every country at the time of publication.

Send money

1. When you're viewing or replying to a message, tap the **App Store** icon next to the compose field and a drawer will slide into view.
2. Slide the panel to the left until the Apple Pay panel appears.
3. Use the buttons to select an amount, then tap Pay.

When you receive money via Apple Pay it's stored within a digital Apple Pay Cash card, which you can see via the Wallet app. This card lets you transfer the money onwards to other people, spend it online using Apple Pay, or deposit it into your bank account - completely free of charge.

If you're asked for money
If a contact requests money from you, tap the amount in the Message chat log or notification panel, then tap Approve to confirm and send the money.

How to return an item bought using Apple Pay
If you've decided that the item you've purchased isn't right and you want to return it, then here's what you need to do:

First, the cashier can use the last four digits of your Device Account Number to find and process the refund. You can find this by going to **Settings** > **Wallet & Apple Pay**, then tap the card. The cashier should be able to do the rest of the work. However, if they need your card details here's what to do:

1. Use the original device you used to make the purchase. That should be your iPhone, but it might also be your Apple Watch.
2. Open the **Wallet** app and select the same card you used to make the purchase.
3. Hold your iPhone near the reader and authorize it using your fingerprint or passcode.

Depending on the store policies, your refund might take a few days to reappear in your bank account.

AirPlay

With AirPlay you can wirelessly stream content to an Apple TV, or play music over AirPlay speakers such as HomePod. All you need to do is connect your iPhone to the same Wi-Fi connection shared with your AirPlay devices; there are no complicated configurations to set up, all the hard work is done for you.

Here's what you can stream to an AirPlay device:

- Music and Beats 1 Radio

Here's what you can stream from the iPhone to the Apple TV:

- Movies and videos
- Music and Beats 1 Radio
- Photos and slideshows
- Third-party video-based apps (such as Netflix or BBC iPlayer)
- Your entire iPhone display

Stream content to your Apple TV

1. Connect your iPhone to the same Wi-Fi connection as the Apple TV.
2. Swipe down from the top-right corner of the screen to access Control Center.
3. You will see a wireless icon in the top-right corner of the playback control window (see image above). Tap on this icon. Alternatively, you can tap on the entire playback window, then after it expands tap the **Airplay** icon in the top-right corner.

4. Choose the Apple TV or AirPlay device.
5. If you've never connected your device to the Apple TV before, enter the 4-character passcode that appears on the TV.

To turn off AirPlay, return to Control Center, tap the **playback** window, tap **AirPlay** then select your device. You can also press the **Back** button on the Apple TV remote.

Control music playback over multiple devices

With multiple AirPlay devices in your home it's possible to play music in two rooms or more at the same time.

To control playback over multiple devices, open Control Center, tap the playback window in the top-right corner then tap the devices you want to use. You can also use Siri by saying something like "*play Green Light in the kitchen*".

Stream a video you're already watching to an Apple TV

While watching a video tap the screen to access playback controls then tap the **AirPlay** button in the bottom-right corner. In the pop-up window, select the Apple TV and you'll start to stream the video.

Mirror your iPhone display

Want to share your iPhone screen on your Apple TV? It's easy, just swipe down from the top-right corner of the screen to access Control Center, tap **Screen Mirroring** then choose the Apple TV.

Your iPhone will immediately begin mirroring its display. While your screen is being mirrored everything you do on the iPhone will appear on-screen, including messages, websites and apps. Note how the images rotates into landscape mode when your turn your device on its side. Also note, that if you view a photo or video while mirroring it will appear full-screen on the TV. To turn off mirroring, just bring Control Center back up then toggle the Mirror switch to Off. Alternatively, lock your iPhone via the power button and the stream will end, or if you have the Apple TV remote to hand press the Back button.

AirDrop

Have you ever wanted to share a photo, note, list video with someone else in the same room? With AirDrop it's possible to wirelessly transfer the file with just a few taps. It works using a combination of Wi-Fi and Bluetooth, and there's no setup required. As a result it's never been quicker or easier to share files with friends, family and colleagues.

Enable AirDrop

To turn on AirDrop go to **Settings** > **General** > **AirDrop**. On the following panel you can enable sharing with those in your Contacts or anyone nearby.

You can also activate or disable AirDrop by using Control Center. To do this swipe down from the top-right corner to access Control Center, press firmly on the top-left box, then when it expands tap the **AirDrop** button. This is what the AirPlay button looks like:

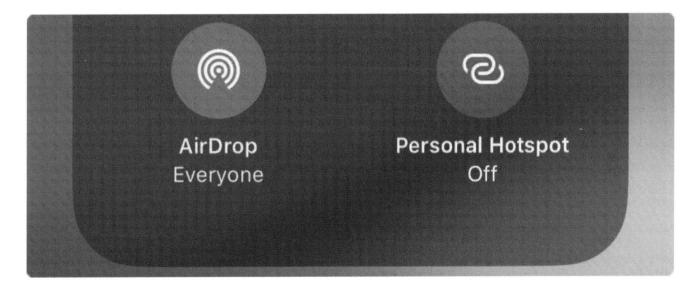

Share a file

AirDrop is now active. To share a file, open a photo, note, web page or anything else with share capabilities, then tap the blue **Share** button at the bottom of the screen. You'll see the AirDrop panel at the top of the Share screen. Anyone nearby with AirDrop enabled will appear in this panel. To share the file with them, just tap on their face or name.

Keyboard

The Multi-Touch keyboard included with iPhone is amazing in several ways. It guesses what word you're trying to write, then automatically finishes it for you. It rotates with the screen to make typing easier. It can detect up to 10 fingertips to make typing quicker. You can hold down a key to see more options, plus much more.

In this tutorial you'll learn how to take full advantage of the on-screen keyboard, including how to turn cap locks on, access emojis, sliding keys and more.

Cap locks

You can enable cap locks by tapping the **Shift** key once, but if you quickly **double-tap** the caps lock key, it will stay enabled. That means you can easily WRITE FULL SENTENCES IN CAPITAL LETTERS.

Slide to type

You can easily add a number by holding your finger on the **123** key, then sliding it to a number that appears. This slide-to-type method also works with capital letters.

Shortcuts

A shortcut is a quick and efficient way to send a common message. So type *"omw"* and your device will automatically write "On my way!" You'll find more shortcuts, plus the ability to create your own, by opening the **Settings** app, then going to **General** > **Keyboard**.

Accents and extra keys

To add accents, extra letters and punctuation, **tap and hold** on a key. You'll see extra options and letters appear above your finger. To select one, simply drag your finger to it then let go.

Predictive Text

Predictive Text attempts to guesses the next word you want to type and then offers it as a one-tap option above the keyboard. To see predictive text in action, open the Messages app and begin to reply to a recipient. As you enter each letter, a series of words will appear above the keyboard that guess what you're trying to type. What makes predictive text really clever is that it learns who you're typing too and changes responses in relation to the person. So if you're talking to a close friend predicted words will be relaxed and fun, but if it's your boss you'll see more formal and serious words appear.

Hide or show the predictive text panel

If you'd like to hide or enable the predictive text panel just open the **Settings** app and go to **General** > **Keyboard** then toggle **Predictive** on or off.

Use QuickType to type with one hand

Let's say you're holding a coffee in one hand, with your iPhone in the other, and you need to quickly reply to a message. With previous versions of iOS you'd need to carefully hold your iPhone and stretch your thumb across the entire screen to reach certain characters. Now, with iOS 12, it's a little bit easier, thanks to QuickType. Here's how it works:

1. While replying to the message or email, tap and hold the **Emoji** (or **Globe**) icon.
2. In the pop-up panel you'll see three keyboard icons appear towards the bottom. These slide the keyboard to either the left-side of the screen, center or right.
3. Slide your finger upwards and select the relevant option, and the keyboard will slide to one side of the screen.

You'll now find it much easier to type with just one hand.

When you want to return the keyboard to it's normal size tap the **arrow** that has appeared next to the keyboard and it will expand back into place.

Emojis

Sometimes it's a great idea to send someone an emoji (picture character). For example hugs, smiley faces and birthdays cakes. To enable emojis, go to **Settings** > **General** > **Keyboard** > **Keyboards** > **Add New Keyboard**. Scroll down the list, then tap **Emoji**. These icons can now be accessed at any time by tapping the emoji key on the keyboard.

Easily move the text cursor

If you'd like to quickly move the text cursor to another word or line press firmly on the keyboard then use it as a trackpad with your finger.

Add a trademark, copyright or registered symbol

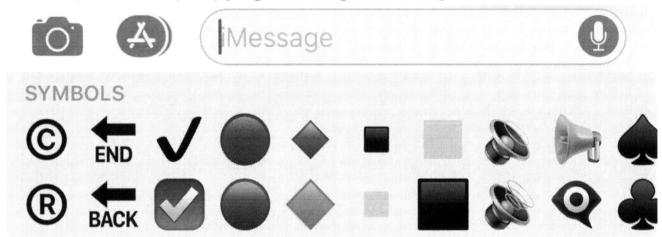

To find the trademark, copyright and registered symbols, open the **Emoji** keyboard then tap the **character** button that's second from the right. Swipe through the emojis a few times and eventually you'll see the trademark, copyright and registered symbols. Tap on one to add it to your text.

Dictate in real-time

To see your words appear as text in real-time, tap the **Microphone** key next to the spacebar then begin to talk out-loud. You'll see your words appear on the screen in real-time.

Turn off lowercase keyboard characters

The standard iPhone keyboard displays lowercase keys, and only swaps to displaying capital letters when the shift key is pressed. If you prefer the traditional setting of always showing capital letters for keys, then open the **Settings** app and go to **General** > **Accessibility** > **Keyboard**, then turn off **Show Lowercase Keys**.

Turn off the character preview when typing

Every time you tap on a letter while typing you'll see a brief pop-up that displays the letter in a larger size. It's helpful when inputting passwords or typing quickly, but if you'd rather switch it off then open the **Settings** app and go to **General** > **Keyboard** and toggle off **Character Preview**.

How to Cut, Copy, & Paste

Copying and pasting is a great way to move text and content from one app to another.

What is copy and paste? It's a way of selecting a piece of text, image or file in one app, then inserting it into another. For example, you could copy your address from Contacts and paste it into Safari, or copy a photo and then paste it into an email. The options are endless.

Copy text

Find a source of text on iPhone, perhaps your phone number in Contacts. **Tap and hold** your finger on the number, let go when the magnifying glass appears and choose **Copy** from the pop-up button.

Paste text

Next, close Contacts and open the Notes app. Create a new note by tapping the plus icon, then **tap and hold** on the empty note and choose **Paste**. Your phone number will appear in the new note.

Select and copy individual pieces of text

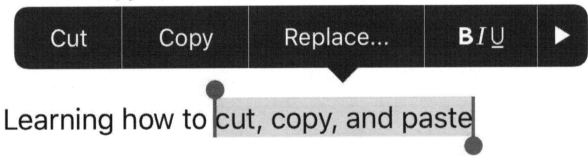

What if you want to copy a line of text from an email? It's easy. Open an email or any other source of lengthy text, then **tap and hold** your finger on a line of text. When the magnifying glass appears, release your finger and you'll see a highlighted area appear on the text. Use the small blue circular handles to select a range of text, then tap the **Copy** button. You can then paste this text into another app or text field.

Cut text

If you tap and hold on an editable piece of text such as a note or email, then you can cut it, as well as copy. What does cut mean? If means the highlighted text is deleted and copied with just one tap. This is an efficient way to move text around apps.

Copy images

To copy an image, simply **tap and hold** on it then choose **Copy** from the pop-up button. You can now paste this image into a new email, SMS or iMessage.

Copy and paste between iOS devices and your Mac

Copying and pasting is a great way to quickly move content from one app to another. With just a few taps it's possible to copy text in Notes then paste it into Safari, or copy an image from the web and paste it into an email. However, it's also possible to copy content from one device to another, and it works effortlessly, almost like magic you could say.

For example, let's copy an image within the Photos app on iPhone, then paste it into an email on iPad. Start by selecting an image in the Photos app, tap **Share** then choose **Copy**. Next, using your iPad compose a new email, **tap and hold** on a blank part of the window then choose **Paste**. In a split second the image will magically appear on iPad.

This process of copying content from one device to another works seamlessly on iPhone, iPad and the Mac, but with one caveat: you need to be signed into the same Apple ID on every device.

Emergency SOS

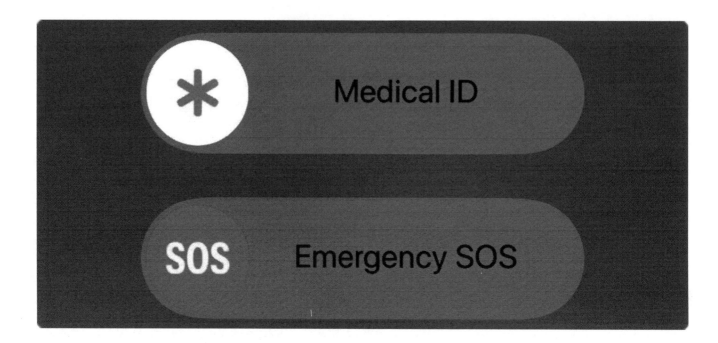

If the worst ever happens and you need to call emergency services, just press the Power and volume up buttons simultaneously, five times, to enable Emergency SOS mode.

When activated you can quickly show your medical ID card or call the emergency services. The Face ID sensor is also deactivated, preventing someone from unlocking your device with your face.

Automatically call the emergency services

If you'd like to automatically call the emergency services whenever SOS mode is activated go to **Settings** > **Emergency SOS** and toggle **Auto Call** on. Now, when you activate Emergency SOS mode a countdown will begin, accompanied by a warning sound, before your iPhone automatically calls the emergency services.

Set up Emergency Contacts

If you would like to notify contacts with an automated message whenever Emergency SOS mode is activated, open the **Health** app, tap **Medical ID** then tap the **Edit** button in the top-right corner of the screen. In the slide-up panel, scroll down, tap add emergency contact and choose someone from your Contacts book.

Apps

Some pretty amazing apps come included with your iPhone, such as Messages, Safari, and Photos, and iOS 12 takes them even further, with new and exciting features. The next set of chapters will reveal the best ways to interact with these apps, and much more.

Messages

Messages is the most commonly used app for iPhone, which perhaps isn't surprising when you consider that more than 2 billion iMessages are sent each day.

In case you've been living under a rock, the Messages app is used to send text messages from one phone to another. But there's so much more. It's also possible to message iPads and Macs, send videos, drawings, animated messages, and even see the location of friends. The Messages app might initially look simple to use, but it's a surprisingly complex and versatile app.

What's an iMessage?

This is a message sent directly from one Apple device to another. iMessages are sent completely free, are automatically encrypted between devices (so no one can read them), can be sent over a Wi-Fi network and can contain video content, photos, audio, and maps. There's also no character or size limit, so your messages can be as long or as complicated as you like. iMessages always appear as blue bubbles in the chat window, while regular SMS messages appear green.

How to send a new message

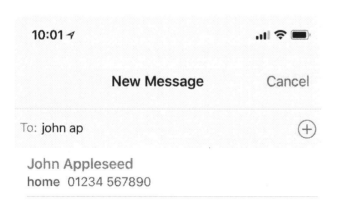

From the home panel of the Messages app, tap the **New Message** icon in the top right corner of the screen. In the **To:** field, begin to type the name of a contact, their email address or a phone number. If the contact already exists on your device then you'll see their name appear above the keyboard. You can tap on this entry to automatically fill the To: field, or continue to enter the recipient's details until complete.

Once you've entered their details in the To: field, tap the text entry field below to begin typing your message. Once it's ready to send just tap the **blue arrow** button above the keyboard and the message will be sent.

Explore the Messages App Drawer

The app drawer within the Messages app lets you do incredible things like share your travel plans, discover a song using Shazam, send stickers, access your food diary and even book a hotel - all within the Messages app.

It's easy to access. Here's how:

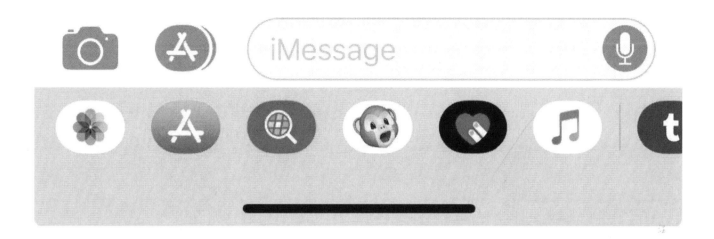

1. When you're viewing or replying to a message, look below the keyboard and you'll find the App Drawer.
2. You'll see several icons, organized in a row. Each represents a different app.
3. Slide the row of apps left or right to scroll through them.
4. Tap on an app icon to use it and share its contents.
5. Tap the **App Store** icon on the far left to explore even more apps for the Messages app.

Take and send a photo or video clip

It's easy enough, just tap the camera icon to the left of the compose field. You'll see a small preview of the camera view appear. To take a photo tap the **small white** icon. To take a video, slow-mo or panorama, pull the preview window to the right then tap **Camera**.

Add a camera effect or filter to your photo or video

If you want to add a filter to a photo, a caption, make an annotation or add a cool effect, then here's how:

1. Tap the **Camera** icon to the left of the message field.
2. Take a photo or video.
3. Tap the **Effects** button in the bottom-left corner.
4. Use the Effects, Edit, or Markup buttons to add effects to your photo or video.
5. Press the white/blue send button to send the photo or video.

That's just a brief overview of how it works. Here's a little more detail about each:

To add a filter to a photo:

Tap on the **Effects** button, tap on **Filters**, then tap on a filter to preview it. You can slide the panel upwards to see all 15 filters.

Add text or speech bubbles:

Tap on the **Effects** button, tap on **Text**, then choose a text style. You can swipe the panel upwards to see all 18 text types. When you've made a selection, you can enter your own text by typing with the keyboard, move the text box around with your finger, or re-size it with two fingers.

To add a shape:

It's similar to above, just tap on the **Effects** button, **Shapes**, then chose from one of the 15 shapes. When you've made a selection, you can enter your own text by typing with the keyboard, move the text box around with your finger, or re-size it with two fingers.

Send a photo from your Library

If you would like to send an existing photo from your library to a friend or family member:

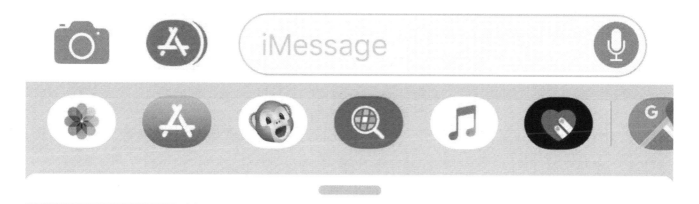

1. Tap the **App Store** icon next to the camera to access App Drawer.
2. Slide it towards the left until you see the **Photos** app icon.
3. Tap this icon to access your photo library
4. Tap on a photo to send it.

If you regularly send photos from your device's library, then it's a good idea to move the Photos app icon to the left of the App Drawer. You can do this by tapping and holding on it, then sliding it where you want it to go.

Send an emoji

Emoji's are awesome. Each one is a beautifully designed graphic that represents a word, emotion or object, and by mixing emoji's with words you can really add emotion or humor to a message.

To send an emoji just tap the **Emoji** button on the keyboard while composing a message. It's at the bottom of the screen next to the spacebar and microphone. You can swipe left and right to scroll through emoji's or tap the grey icons at the bottom of the screen to jump to a theme.

Send an Animoji

With both iPhone XS and XS Max, you can create and send animated emojis using your face. Animojis track more than 50 facial movements and can be used to create amazing animated expressions. To create and send an Animoji:

1. When you're viewing or replying to a message, tap the **App Store** icon next to the compose field and a drawer will slide into view.
2. Tap the **Animoji** icon. It's third from the left next to Apple Pay.
3. You'll immediately see the Animoji come to life on the screen as it mirrors your facial expressions and head movements.
4. To navigate through the different Animojis, slide the panel of faces on the left-side of the screen, You can also tap on an Animoji to see all of them at once.
5. Tap the **record** button, and the Animoji will start recording. Say your message out-loud and play around with expressions.
6. After you're done tap the **record** button to end. You'll see a preview of the recording. To send the Animoji, just tap the blue **Send** button.

Create your very own Memoji

Sending a video message of your face is so 2017, because with the new Memoji feature in iOS 12, you can now create your very own 3D avatar, then use it to send fun animated messages to friends and family. Here's how it works:

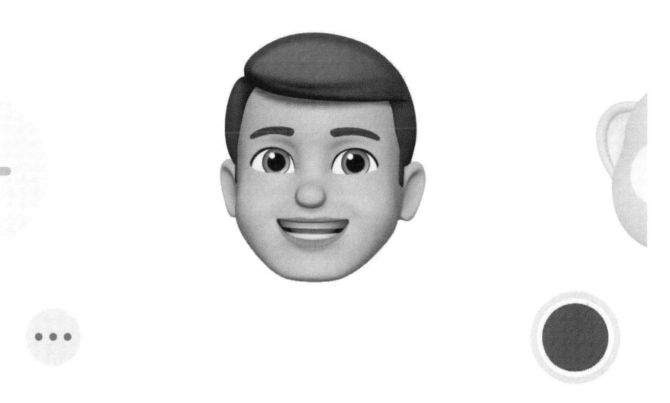

1. Start by opening the **Messages** app.
2. Tap on the **Animoji** button (the icon shows a monkey face)
3. Tap the **+** button at the bottom of the list, or in the upper-left corner of the Animoji panel.
4. Use the creation tool to create your very own Memoji.
5. Tap **Done** in the top-right corner to save and use your new Memoji.

Let's take a more detailed look at some of the Memoji options available:

Skin colors

Memojis start life with yellow skin, but you're given 17 other colors to choose from including green, blue, or purple. Once you select a skin color, you can adjust it even further using an on-screen slider.

Freckles

While choosing a skin color, you can also choose from three types of freckles.

Hairstyle

Next up is hairstyle. There's a wealth of options to choose from, and as you might expect, each hairstyle can be chosen with one of 15 different colors. You can even add highlights to your hair.

Headshape

Choose from a selection of head shapes, including age and chine.

Eyes, eyelashes and brows

Select from 9 eye shapes, 9 eyelash designs, and 15 types of eyebrow.

Nose and Lips

Whatever shape nose you have, you'll find the corresponding shape here in the Memoji creator. You can also pick from a range of lip shapes, and go all-out on the lip color, with 7 basic choices, then an extended color picker for those looking for an exacting shade.

Ears

The Memoji creator includes a large selection of ear types to choose from, and you can even add earrings and studs – each with its own custom color.

Facial Hair

The Memoji creator comes with 3 types of facial hair: moustache, beard, and sideburn. There are dozens to choose from, and of course, they can each be customized using color.

Eyewear

Whether you wear glasses or sunglasses, you'll find a large amount of eyewear types to choose from. You can even change the lens color using a secondary control.

Headwear

Choose from hats, skullcaps, shawls and more, using the Headwear picker. As standard, they come in a fetching light grey, but you can add color to each.

Replace your head with an Memoji or Animoji

If you want to really surprise someone, then sending a photo or video of yourself with your face replaced with an Memoji, is a good way to do that. What's particularly impressive is that the Memoji matches your head movements perfectly. There's even a subtle shadow below to make it look almost realistic.

Here's how it works:

1. Tap the **Camera** icon to the left of the message field.

2. Tap the **Effects** button in the bottom-left corner.
3. Tap the **Animoji** button.
4. Choose a Memoji (it works best if the Memoji looks like you).
5. Press the small **X** button to close the Animoji panel.
6. Pose, then take a photo.
7. Press the **white/blue** button to send your snap.

Automatically turn words into emoji's

So you've composed a message, but you want to liven it up with some fun emoji's. It's surprisingly easy, thanks to a clever feature that automatically scans your message for emoji-related words then lets you replace them with a tap of a finger. Here's how:

So I'm thinking of ordering pizza, don't they use bikes to deliver?

FOOD & DRINK

1. Compose a message with some emoji-friendly words (think *"happy"*, *"fireworks"*, *"pizza"* etc).
2. Tap the **emoji** button on the keyboard. Any emoji-friendly words will glow gold.
3. Tap on the gold words that you'd like to replace with emoji's and they will automatically swap from text to emoji graphics.

Send a drawing

The Messages app enables you to draw a message and send it with just a few taps of your finger. It's a surprisingly fun process with endless appeal. Here's how it works:

1. When you're viewing or replying to a message, tap the **App Store** icon next to the compose field and a drawer will slide into view.
2. Slide the panel to the left until the draw panel appears. It looks like two fingertips over a heart.
3. Start to draw on the black panel in the bottom half of the screen. You'll see your drawing come to life under your fingertip.
4. Once you've finished tap the **blue arrow** icon to send the drawing.

Send a Digital Touch effect

Using the Messages app, it's possible to send a Digital Touch effect like a fireball, kiss or heartbeat. There are six effects to choose from, here's how they work:

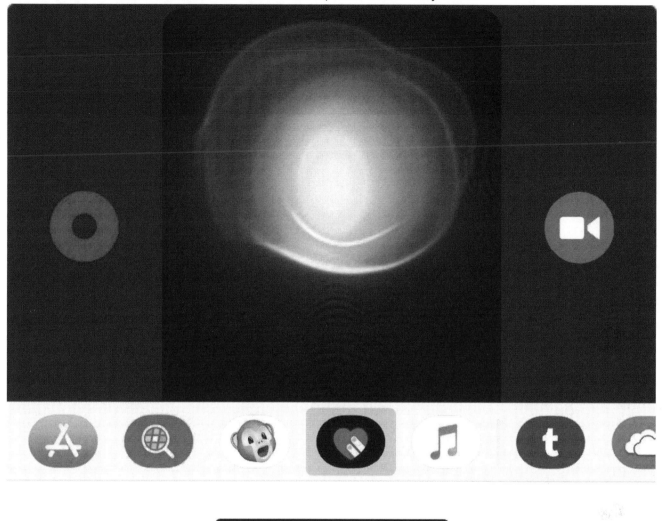

1. **Drawing**. Covered in the previous tutorial, simply scribble on the black panel to draw.
2. **Taps**. Simply tap anywhere on the black preview panel with your finger and an animated tap will appear.
3. **Fireball**. Press and hold on the screen with your finger. When you let go a fireball effect will be sent to the contact.
4. **Kiss**. Tap with two fingers and you'll send a kiss message.
5. **Heartbeat**. Tap and hold on the screen and an animated heartbeat will be sent.
6. **Broken heart**. Tap and hold with two fingers then slide downwards to send a broken heart effect to the recipient.

Send a photo or video with hand drawn graphics

Want to send a cheeky photo or video with a hand-drawn annotation? It's both fun and easy using the Messages app. Here's how it works:

1. When you're viewing or replying to a message, tap the App Store icon next to the compose field and a drawer will slide into view.
2. Tap the Digital Touch icon. It looks like a heart with two fingers over it.
3. Tap the camera icon towards the right of the screen, then take a photo or video of yourself.
4. Draw on the screen using your finger. You can swap between colors using the shortcuts at the top of the screen. Tap and hold on one of these colors and you'll access a palette wheel.
5. Tap the small blue arrow in the bottom corner to send the annotated image, or tap the back arrow in the upper-left corner to take another photo.

Send a handwritten message

Want to send a personal handwritten message? Just rotate your iPhone into landscape mode while composing a message and a large white panel will appear. Draw or write onto this panel using your finger and you'll see a beautiful handwritten message appear. Tap **Done** when you're ready to send the message or tap the arrow on the right to add a second handwritten message. You'll also see thumbnails of pre-composed messages at the bottom of the screen. Tap on one to preview it or swipe the panel to the left to see more.

Send a message with an animated effect

If you'd like to emphasize a message with an animated effect such as slam dunk or whisper then it's easy using iOS. Four effects are included in the Messages app: a slam dunk, loud shout, gentle whisper or invisible ink – where the recipient must swipe their finger across the message to reveal it. Here's how to send a message with an animated effect:

1. Compose your text, then instead of tapping the blue send arrow press firmly on it.
2. In the pop-up window, tap one of the four options on the right-side of the screen to see a preview of how it looks.
3. Once you're happy with an effect, tap the **blue arrow** to send the message.

Send a full-screen effect with your message

Want to really grab someone's attention with a message? Try sending a full-screen effect. With the Messages app you can include one of nine effects that take over the screen for a brief moment:

- **Echo**. Your message is repeated across the screen hundreds of times.
- **Spotlight**. A brief spotlight appears on your message.
- **Balloons**. A flurry of balloons floats up the screen.
- **Confetti**. Great for celebratory messages!
- **Inflatable heart**. A love balloon floats up the screen.
- **Lasers**. A techno laser streaks across the screen.
- **Fireworks**. Explosive fireworks erupt across the screen.
- **Shooting star**. A blue shooting star flies across the screen then explodes.
- **Sparks**. Glittering gold sparks fall down the screen.

Here's how to send a full-screen effect:

1. Type your message, then instead of tapping the blue send arrow press firmly on it.
2. Tap the **Screen** tab at the top of the screen, then select an effect by swiping to the left with your finger.
3. Once you've found an effect tap the **blue arrow** button to send the message.

Add a Tapback sticker to messages

If you want to add a personal touch to a delivered message just **tap and hold** on the message bubble to see six stickers that can be attached and seen by the recipient.

See the details of a contact

Need to see the phone number or address of the person you're chatting too? Tap their **thumbnail** image (or initials) at the top of the chat window and you'll see their details, shortcuts for messaging or calling the contact, the ability to share your location or a button for turning on Do Not Disturb – which prevents your phone from initiating a notification when the contact gets in touch. Scroll down and you'll see any images and attachments shared between yourself and the contact.

Add a new contact to your phone

If you receive a message from a new contact and you'd like to save them to your phone then tap their avatar at the top of the screen (it will probably look like a grey thumbnail) then tap **Create New Contact**. If your phone thinks it knows who the person is then it will suggest a name beneath the avatar thumbnail.

Share your current location

Meeting a friend somewhere in town? If they're having trouble finding you, tap the blue Info button in the top right corner of the chat window, then tap the **Send My Current Location** button. This will instantly send your location on a map to the recipient, enabling them to track you down with ease.

Hide alerts from a contact or thread

If you're being spammed with messages, or you just want some peace and quiet from a group conversation, then it's easy to mute them and prevent any further notifications.

If you're already viewing the conversation thread, tap on the persons thumbnail (or initial) at the top of the screen, then in the following panel toggle **Hide Alerts** on.

Alternatively, from the home page of Messages, slide the conversation thread to the left and tap **Hide Alerts**.

When Hide Alerts is turned on you'll see a moon crescent icon next to the person or group. Now, whenever they send you a message you will not receive any notifications. You will, however, still see a red badge over the Messages app icon.

Delete a conversation

There are two ways to remove chat conversations from the Messages app. The simplest is to **swipe right-to-left** across the chat conversation from the home page of the Messages app. You'll see a red button marked **Delete** slide into view, just tap it to clear the conversation from your device:

Alternatively, tap the **Edit** button at the top of the Messages screen, then tap the conversation/s that you wish to delete. Once you've made your selection tap the blue Delete button in the bottom corner.

Start a group conversation

Why talk to only one person at a time, when you can join in on the fun of a group chat? To start a group conversation, tap the **New message** icon in the top right corner of the screen, then enter the name first recipient into the **To:** field. Next, either tap the **plus** icon or type another name into the **To:** field. You can enter as many recipients as you like. If you add someone by accident just tap their name then hit the **delete** button on the keyboard.

How to leave a conversation

If you need to leave a group conversation tap the blue **Info** button in the top-right corner of the chat window, swipe down then tap the **Leave this Conversation** button.

See when a message was sent

Here's a great tip that goes unnoticed by most: to see the exact time a message was sent or received, **slide the chat window to the left** using your finger. You'll see the chat bubbles slide to one side and the time each was sent/received appear.

Automatically delete messages after 30 days/1 year

You can tell Messages to automatically remove chats, photos and more after either 30 days or 1 year. To activate this feature, go to **Settings** > **Messages** > **Keep Messages.**

Keep video and audio messages

By default, audio and video messages are automatically deleted after 2 minutes. To keep them forever, go to **Settings** > **Messages**, then scroll down where you'll see separate options for storing both audio and video messages.

Safari

Safari is the very best way to browse the web on your iPhone. It's blazingly fast, rendering web pages in an instant. It supports Apple Pay, so you can make purchases on the web without entering your credit card details. It can strip all the ads and junk out of a page to show you only the content you want to see, it automatically blocks pop-ups and so much more.

Entering web URLs

apple.com — Apple Cancel

Top Hit

Apple
apple.com

Open Safari for the first time and you'll see it's in-built bookmarks and the address field at the top of the screen. To visit a website, just tap on the address field and enter an URL via the on-screen keyboard. Tap the blue **Go** button on the keyboard to visit the site.

Searching the web

The address bar in Safari also acts as a search engine, so to search the web for any question or search term, just type your query into the address bar at the top of the screen. As you type into the address bar, notice that Safari offers search suggestions in real-time. Tap on a suggestion or the blue **Go** button on the keyboard to confirm your query. You'll then see results appear on Google's website.

Show the control panel

While browsing the web Safari will automatically hide the control panel at the bottom of the screen. This gives web pages more room to show content and images, but it makes going back a page or accessing tabs and bookmarks more difficult. To quickly restore the control panel, tap anywhere along the bottom of the screen. You'll see the panel slide back into place.

Go back a page

Here's a great Multi-Touch tip: to go back to the last page, swipe your finger from the very left side of the screen inwards. You'll see the previous page appear beneath the current one, and with any luck it won't have to reload itself. You can also go forward a page by swiping inwards from the right.

Tabs

Tabs make it possible to have more than one website open at a time. This is useful for when you need to keep a page open for reference while reading another, or for quickly accessing a site on regular occasions.

To access the tabs view, tap the **tabs** button in the very bottom right corner of the screen...

You'll see the current page zoom and angle downwards, and a selection of buttons will appear at the bottom of the screen. Tap the **plus icon** to open an additional tab. To close a tab, tap the small **x** button in its top left corner, or swipe the tab window to the left using your finger.

iCloud tabs

Using iCloud it's possible to sync tabs across all your devices. Tabs are automatically synced using your Apple ID. To access them tap the **tabs** button in the bottom right corner of the screen, then push the current tabs upwards. You'll see a list of iCloud tabs slide up from the bottom of the screen.

Use Apple Pay to make a purchase online

If you see the Apple Pay button at the checkout, tap it to pay for your item/s without using a credit card.

Apple Pay requires a valid credit card. If you haven't already set one up, go to **Settings > Wallet & Apple Pay > Add Credit or Debit Card** and follow the on-screen instructions.

Once you're ready to make a purchase, tap the **Pay** button, then hold your iPhone in front of your face. In an instant your purchase will complete.

Use Safari Reader to remove clutter on web pages

Browsing the web can be tricky when the page is cluttered with ads or unformatted for mobile devices. To make reading in Safari easier, tap the **Reader View** icon in the left corner of the address bar to remove adverts and distractions. Tap it again to return to the regular version of the page.

Customize Safari Reader settings

While using Safari Reader, it's possible to tweak the font, background color and text size. To do this just tap the **aA** icon in the address bar, then tweak the on-screen settings to suit your taste.

Search a web page for text

Looking for a keyword, name or figure on a web page? By pressing the **Share** button, then tapping **Find on Page**, you can search a web page for anything text-based.

Block ads and junk from slowing down the web

Using Safari it's possible to install "extensions" which prevent adverts from loading on web pages. With less content and scripting to load, web pages will appear faster, use less memory and require less bandwidth.

To install and active a content blocker, open the App Store and search for "content blocker". There are quite a few to choose from, and some are priced while others are free. It's worth doing some research beforehand, but once you've chosen an app install it then go to **Settings > Safari > Content Blockers** and toggle the content blocker app "on".

Enable Private Browsing

You can browse the web without saving any history, searches, passwords or field entries by enabling Private Browsing mode. To do this, tap the **Tabs** button in the bottom right corner then tap the **Private** button. Safari will ask if you would like to keep the existing window/s open or close them. Tap whichever option is relevant to your needs. You'll then notice the Safari interface change color from white to grey. To disable Private Browsing mode, re-open the tabs window then tap the Private button again.

Change the default search engine

By default, Safari searches the web using results from Google. This is probably the best option for most users, but if you'd rather search using Yahoo! or Bing, go to **Settings > Safari > Search Engine**. From the following panel you can change the default search engine.

Share a page

Sometimes it's helpful to share a website with friends and family. Safari offers a wealth of sharing options, including the ability to email web pages, send an URL via the messages app, share a site onto Twitter and Facebook, wirelessly beam a page to others sharing the same Wi-Fi connection and much more.

To access these sharing abilities, tap the **Share** icon at the bottom of the screen (it looks like a square with an arrow pointing upwards out of it). You'll see the share panel slide up the screen, with icons and shortcuts to each sharing ability. Tap on whichever is most suitable for your needs.

Quickly type domain addresses

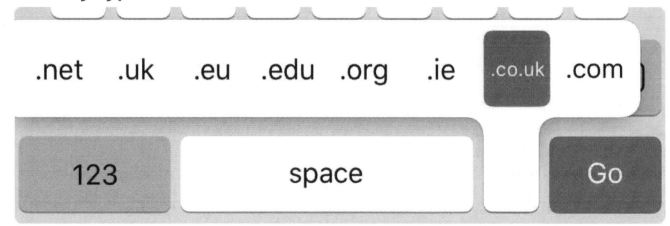

There's no need to manually type .com, .co.uk or many of the other common domain addresses. Instead, touch and hold the **full-stop key** on the keyboard to choose from a variety of .com and other suffixes.

Turn on pop-ups

Pop-ups are the bane of browsing the web, often taking the form of full-screen adverts that beg for your attention. Safari automatically blocks pop-ups from appearing on your device, but you can turn them on by going to **Settings** > **Safari**, then toggling off the **Block Pop-ups** button.

View desktop versions of websites

Once a website has finished loading, tap the **Share** button at the bottom of the screen, swipe the lower panel to the left then tap the **Request Desktop Site** button. The page will then re-load and (if applicable) show the desktop layout and design.

How to scan a credit card with the camera

Entering numbers and details using a touch screen is always a chore, but iOS makes things slightly easier. When you're at the checkout of a website and ready to input your credit card details, you'll see an option above the keyboard that says "Scan Credit Card". Tap this button and the back-facing camera will turn on, with a rectangle in the center of the screen. Place the front of your credit card in this rectangle and your device will automatically read the numbers and expiry dates before inputting them into the website.

Clear your web browsing history and cookies

If you need to clear your browsing history, go to **Settings** > **Safari** then tap the **Clear History** button. This cannot be undone, so only tap this button if you're sure that you wish to erase your recent browsing history.

Similarly, from the same Settings panel you can also clear cookies and data. Cookies are small pieces of data stored in Safari that tell a website of your previous activity on the site.

Save a webpage as a PDF

If you use your iPhone in a work environment then chances are you'll need work with PDF's every now and then. They're great for presentations, print nicely and support a wide variety of layouts.

Using iOS, you can save entire web pages as PDF's, then share them with friends or colleagues. Here's how:

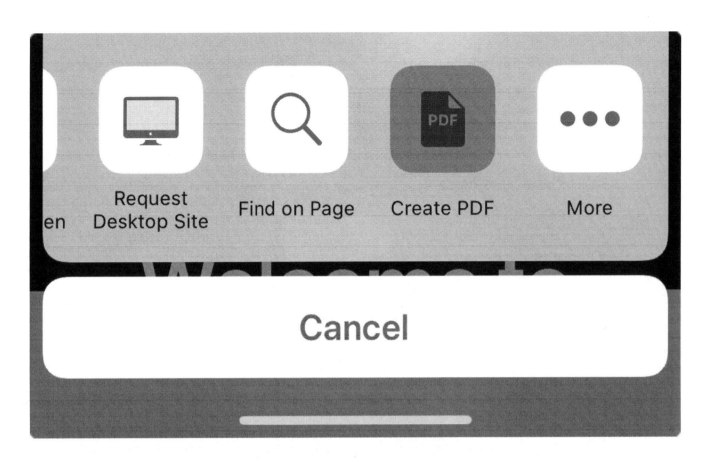

1. Use Safari to visit the web page you wish to convert to PDF
2. Tap the **Share** button, then choose **CreatePDF**.
3. Use the edit sheet to add notes, annotations and share options.

Mail

Alongside the Messages app, Mail must come close to being on the most used apps on iPhone. That's because unlike Facebook or Twitter, there's simply no way to avoid having an email address — it's a basic requirement of using the web.

Thankfully, the Mail app on iOS is brilliant. It's designed with a clean, white interface that helps you focus on what's important: your emails. Buttons are colored blue, and basic Multi-Touch gestures enable you to delete messages, flag them and more.

Add an iCloud email account

10:40 ✈

< Accounts   **Add Account**

Adding an iCloud or MobileMe email account is delightfully simple:

1. Begin by opening the **Settings** app, then tap on the **Passwords & Accounts** button.
2. Tap on the **Add Account** button, then select the **iCloud** button at the top of the screen.
3. Your device will ask for the Apple ID and Password associated with iCloud or MobileMe account. Simply enter these and tap **Next**, or if you don't have an Apple ID yet, you can sign up for one by tapping the **Get a Free Apple ID** button at the bottom of the screen.
4. Your device will verify your Apple ID details. Once the process has completed, you can choose whether to sync your Mail, Contacts, photos and more – all via iCloud.

Congratulations, you are now ready to send and receive emails.

Add a Gmail/Yahoo/Hotmail account

If you already have a Gmail, Hotmail, AOL, Microsoft Exchange or Yahoo email account, then it's easy to set it up on iOS. With just a few taps of your finger you can send and receive emails using the elegant and magical Mail app.

1. To get started, open the **Settings** app then select the **Passwords & Accounts** button.
2. Next, tap on the **Add Account** button and select your email service from the list displayed on-screen.
3. Your device will ask for the username and password associated with your email account. Simply enter these and tap **Next**.
4. Your device will verify your mail account details. Once the process has completed you can choose whether you wish to sync mail, contacts and notes.

Add a custom email account

If you have a custom email account – perhaps associated with work or a personal website - then it's possible to enter its details and access your messages through the Mail app. Adding an account isn't as easy as simply entering a username and password, you'll also need the server details and choose whether to use IMAP or POP3 (explained shortly).

1. To get started, open the **Settings** app and go to **Passwords & Accounts** > **Add Account**, then tap the **Other** button and then choose **Add Mail Account**.
2. In the Name field, enter the name you wish recipients to see when they receive your email. Next, enter your email address and password used to access your account. In the Description field, enter a mail account name that's easily recognizable.
3. Tap **Next** and your device will attempt to verify the account. It will then ask you to choose an IMAP or POP account type. IMAP accounts store emails on a server, enabling you to check your email from multiple sources, i.e. your iPhone and Mac. A POP account stores emails locally on your device, meaning the account can only be accessed from that device.
4. Under Host Name, enter the server address for your email account. It might be something like imap.example.com. Next, enter your username once again in the User Name field, the outgoing server address and your password if required. Click Next and your device will verify the account.
5. If everything is correct, then you'll be ready to send and receive emails from your email account.

Format text in an email

If you'd like to bold, italicize or underline a word or sentence while composing an email, highlight the text then tap on the option arrow. Next, tap BIU and select the format you wish to use.

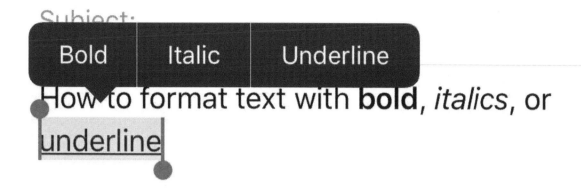

Attach images and videos with emails

Want to attach an image or two with an email? Begin by composing an email, then tap and hold on the screen. When the pop-up window appears above your finger tap the right arrow then choose **Insert Photo or Video**. Your photos will slide into view, so simply select an image then tap Choose to attach the photo.

Print an email

To print an email, tap the **Share** button at the bottom of the screen then tap **Print**. Select a wireless printer from the following panel (it must be connected to the same Wi-Fi connection as your device), then tap Print.

Annotate a photo or PDF

While replying to an email with an image or PDF attachment, you can tap and hold on the file then choose Markup and Reply to add sketches, shapes, a signature and text.

There are some really clever features included with Markup. For example, while annotating try drawing a basic shape, then in the pop-up window at the bottom of the screen choose the polygonal version of it to make a perfect shape. You can also customize the thickness of lines by tapping the line button on the right-side of the screen, or enable a magnifying glass to get a better look at your annotations.

Search your emails

Looking for an email that's buried away? Just tap on the **Search** field at the top of the screen to search by name, subject or content. The search field is available from every window in the Mail app. If you can't see it just pull the screen down with your finger.

Save a draft email

While composing an email, drag the top title bar downwards to temporarily hide the draft message. This enables you to continue reading emails and exploring your inboxes. To return to the draft email, just tap on its title bar at the bottom of the screen.

Delete an email with a single swipe

Erasing emails can become a chore, so to speed up the process, simply **swipe your finger right-to-left** across the email message while in the Inbox. Swipe quickly and the email will be deleted instantly.

More email options

After swiping an email from right-to-left, tap the More button and you'll see a selection of controls slide up from the bottom of the screen. Most of them are self explanatory, but by tapping Move Message... you can store an email in a folder separate to the inbox, and by tapping Notify Me you can get a notification when someone replies to the email thread - handy if you're waiting for an important email to arrive.

Flag an email

After swiping right-to-left across an email, tap the **Flag** button to highlight the email in your inbox. The highlight appears as a small orange circle to the left of the message, but if you haven't opened the message yet it appears as a blue circle surrounded by an orange circle. You can un-flag the message by swiping across it and choosing **Unflag**.

See only unread emails

Email is messy, it takes time to sort through and our inboxes are often littered with junk. To make life just that little bit easier, you can sort your inbox to show only unread messages by tapping the **Unread** button in the bottom-left corner of the screen.

Delete multiple emails

While viewing your inbox, tap the blue **Edit** text in the top right corner. You'll see every email slide to the right slightly, and a pale empty dot appear alongside them. Next, tap on the messages you'd like to delete (you can select as many as you like), you'll see them become highlighted by blue ticks. Once you're happy with the selection, tap the **Delete** button at the bottom of the screen.

Move or mark multiple emails

Follow the steps above, but instead of deleting the selected messages select either Mark or Move at the bottom of the screen. Mark enables you to flag the messages, mark them as unread or move them to the Junk folder. Move enables you to store the emails in a separate folder from the Inbox.

See the contact details of an email

While reading an email, tap on the **name** of the contact at the top of the message and you'll see their details in full. These include the authors email, and if they've attached it their address and contact details.

Get email reply notifications

Waiting for an important reply to an email? With iOS it's possible to receive a notification when the reply arrives. To enable it, open the email, tap the **Flag** button, then tap **Notify Me...**

Save a contact to your device

If you'd like to save an emails contact details to your Device, then tap on their name while reading an email then select either **Create New Contact** or **Add to Existing Contact**. This will add their email address and any other information saved with the email to the Contacts book on your device.

Add an event to your Calendar

11:33

 ❮ All Inboxes

 **Siri found 1 Event**
Sun 13 May at 15:00 add... ⊗

Whenever you receive an email about flights, bookings or invitations, Siri will automatically offer to add the details to your Calendar. To confirm this action, tap the small **add** button in the Siri bar above the email.

Unsubscribe from mailing lists with just a tap

If you accidentally subscribed to a mailing list and no longer want to receive unsolicited messages then the Mail app makes it incredibly easy to unsubscribe. Here's how:

1. Open the **Mail** app on your device and select an email from a mailing list that you wish to unsubscribe from.
2. Tap **Unsubscribe** at the top of the email, then tap **Unsubscribe** again in the pop-up message.

The Mail app will automatically message the mailing list to remove you from its list, which means you should never have to scroll down to the bottom of a mailing list email, tap the unsubscribe button and fill out a form.

Phone

The iPhone might include the word "phone" in its name, but that doesn't mean it's used primarily as a telephone. In fact, there are many iPhone users who have never made or taken a call on their device, instead of using the device as a fully fledged computer for sharing media, browsing the web and playing games.

Nevertheless, the Phone app is still an essential in-built feature. One that's simple to use and easy to use. This book could cover the basics such as making a call or accessing the keypad, but those features are so easy anyone can intuitively pick them up. Instead, let's take a look at some phone-related tips that often go unnoticed.

Add a photo to a contact

By assigning a photo to a contact you can visually see who's calling. It's also a fun way to spruce up your contacts book. To do this:

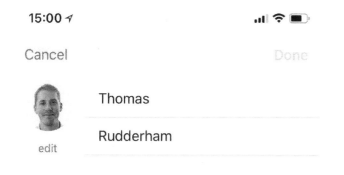

1. Open the **Contacts** app.
2. Select a contact then tap the **Edit** button.
3. Tap the circular **add photo** button.
4. You'll see options for taking a photo on the spot, or choosing one from your library. Select whichever is relevant, then scale and position the image so that the contact's face is in the center of the preview panel.
5. Once you're happy with the image, tap **Choose** to assign the photo to the contact.

Dial a number using Siri

If you'd rather dictate a number than tap each key, open Siri by pressing the **Power** button twice then say *"Call..."* followed by the number or contact name. Siri will then dial the contact automatically.

Turn off Data Roaming

When traveling abroad your phone will piggy-back on a local carrier to enable you to make calls, send messages and browse the web. This often means that you have to pay extra for each megabyte of data used, and the prices can be shockingly high. To prevent a shock when the next bill arrives, go to **Settings** > **Mobile Data** > **Mobile Data Options**, and de-toggle the **Data Roaming** switch. This will prevent your phone from downloading data while abroad, although you'll still be able to make phone calls and send/receive plain SMS messages.

See your mobile data usage

Most network carriers limit your data usage each month. It might be 1GB, 500MB or even less. Go over that limit and you might be charged extra. To see your usage, go to **Settings** > **Mobile Data** and scroll down to the **MOBILE DATA** panel.

MOBILE DATA

Current Period	165 GB
Current Period Roaming	8.6 GB
1Blocker 1.3 MB	⬤
Activity 130 MB	⬤

From there you'll see the total data used during the lifetime of your contract, plus the amount used in the current period/month.

Respond to calls with text messages

Too busy to take a call? If so it's possible to answer calls with a pre-set text message. To do this, go to **Settings** > **Phone** > **Respond with Text**. You can enter up to three messages by tapping on each greyed-out field. Now, when someone calls, tap the Message button and choose one of the pre-set messages that you've entered.

Forward calls to another number

To forward all incoming calls to another number, go to **Settings** > **Phone** > **Call Forwarding,** then toggle the switch on. In the following pane enter the number you wish calls to transfer too, then tap the **Back** button.

When Call Forwarding is enabled you'll see the forwarding icon appear in the menu bar next to the signal strength. To turn Call Forwarding off, simply de-toggle the switch in the Call Forwarding Settings panel.

Block numbers

If you're being pestered by an unknown number and want to block it, open the **Phone** app, tap **Recents** then tap the small **info** icon next to the number you wish to block. In the following panel tap **Block this Caller** and they won't be able to annoy you again.

You can also block numbers from the **Settings** app by going to **Phone** > **Blocked**. Next, tap the **Add New...** button and select a contact from your phone.

Unblock a contact

To remove someone from your blocked list, go to **Settings** > **Phone** > **Blocked** and swipe from right to left across the contacts name, then tap **Unblock**.

Turn off your caller ID

If you'd like to remain anonymous when making a call, go to **Settings** > **Phone** > **Show My Caller ID** then de-toggle the switch. From now on, whenever you make a call your number and name will remain hidden.

Assign a custom ringtone to a contact

Assigning a custom ringtone to a contact is one of the easiest ways to instantly tell who's trying to get in touch, and it's possible to select from a variety of custom tones, as well as purchase and download ringtones based upon the latest music in the charts. It's a quick and easy process, taking only seconds to complete.

1. Begin by opening the **Contacts** app, then select the contact you'd like to assign a custom ringtone.
2. Tap the blue **Edit** button in the top right corner of the screen, then tap the **Ringtone** button. You can now choose from a wide selection of audio tones that suit the particular contact.
3. If you prefer the older ringtones that were introduced with the very first iPhone and used through to the iPhone 5, then tap the **Classic** button at the bottom of the ringtones list. From the following panel you can select a classic tone from years gone by.
4. If you'd like to assign a music track as a tone, tap the **Buy More Tones** button at the top of the Ringtone screen. You'll then be taken to the Tones section of the iTunes Store, where you can preview and download a number of ringtones based upon contemporary and classical music.

FaceTime

With FaceTime, you can be with friends and family at any time and place. Whether it's a birthday, anniversary, meeting or just a chat, FaceTime lets you be a part of the moment with crystal clear video and audio.

FaceTime works over Wi-Fi, and enables you to call another iPhone, iPad, iPod touch or a Mac. The recipient will receive an alert that's just like a phone call, and with just one tap of a finger, you're connected.

Make a FaceTime call

Open the **FaceTime** app and sign in if you haven't used it before. You'll see your contacts listed down the middle of the screen. Tap a contact to automatically begin calling them, or tap the info icon to see more options.

Call from Contacts

You can also select a contact from the Phone or Contacts app, then call them via FaceTime from there.

Swap cameras

By default, FaceTime uses the front-facing camera. However, if you'd like to show your contact something happening in front of you, simply tap the **camera swap** button at the bottom of the screen.

Disable your camera or mute the microphone

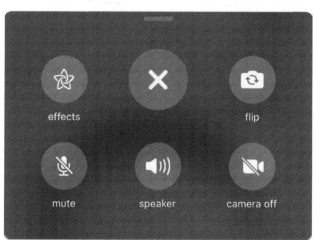

If you need to briefly hide your camera view, or disable your audio, then tap the **Options** button in the bottom-right corner then tap **camera off.** You can also mute your audio from this panel too. If you don't want to be seen at all, then it's probably better to make a FaceTime Audio call instead.

Add stickers and filters to your face

While making a FaceTime call, you can add a filter to a photo, a caption, make an annotation or add a cool effect. Here's how:

1. During the FaceTime call, tap the **Effects** button in the bottom-left corner.
2. Use the **Filters**, **Text**, or **Shapes** buttons to add effects to your photo or video.
3. Notice how the effect follows the movement of your face.

Use a Memoji to replace your head

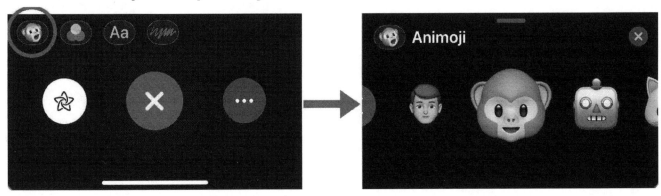

If you want to be a little crazy, then it's possible to replace your head with a Memoji in real-time. To do this:

1. During the FaceTime call, tap the **Effects** button in the bottom-left corner.
2. Tap on the **Animoji** icon, then select either a Memoji or one of the existing Animojis.

Move your image around

You can move the preview portrait of yourself around the screen using your finger. Helpful if there's something you need to see that's being blocked by your own face.

Add a favorite

When not making a FaceTime call, tap the Favorites button at the bottom of the screen to add a contact into the favorites list. You can add contacts by tapping the plus icon in the top right corner.

Start a group call

With iOS 12, it's now possible to talk to up to 32 people at once using FaceTime. If you're worried about that being a bit chaotic, then FaceTime tries to alleviate the issue by showing whoever is speaking front and center, with everyone else zoomed back into smaller thumbnail windows.

The easiest way to start a group call is actually via the Messages app. Here's how it works:

1. Use the Messages app to start a group conversation. This is actually a pretty good way to schedule or plan a meeting, and invite everyone who needs to be there.
2. Once you're ready to start the call, tap on the group name at the top of the screen (you should see small thumbnail of their faces), then tap the **FaceTime** option.
3. If everyone has iOS 12, then the whole group should appear in the FaceTime call.
4. You can also invite people to a FaceTime group call by tapping on the **Options** button in the bottom-right corner of the screen.
5. If you would like to zoom into someone, just tap on their thumbnail.

Music

The Music app has always been the best way to listen to music on iPhone. It has a beautiful interface, access to millions of tracks via Apple Music, exclusive TV shows, curated playlists, videos, top charts and Beats 1 Radio.

There's a limitless source of music available in Apple Music, but it comes at a price: to access the full service you'll need to pay a monthly subscription. It's priced slightly differently for each country but roughly works out about the same as a large takeaway pizza. For anyone who listens to the latest charts, streams music on a daily basis or has a wide variety of music tastes, it's definitely worth the asking price. For everyone else, Apple Music still offers Beats 1 Radio, the ability to follow artists and preview music.

Browse Apple Music

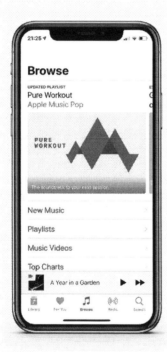 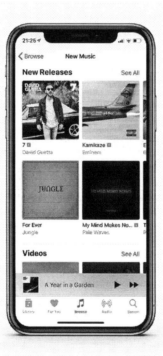 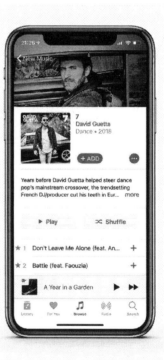

It couldn't be simpler to find the latest tracks in Apple Music, just open the **Music** app then tap the **Browse** button at the bottom of the screen. From here you'll find the latest tracks, albums and videos. You can also search Apple Music for any artist, track or album. To do this tap the search button in the bottom corner. By default the Music app searches your own library, but you can search Apple Music by tapping the **Apple Music** tab.

Add music to your Library

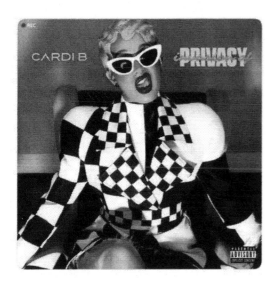

Invasion of Privacy
Cardi B
Hip-Hop/Rap • 2018

If there's a track or album that you'd like to save locally for offline listening, start playing to it then tap the **+Add** button at the top of the screen. The track or album will then be added to your device. If you'd like to download all the tracks for offline listening just tap the iCloud icon.

Automatically download music to your device

If you'd like to automatically download music to your device whenever you add a new album or track to your library then open the **Settings** app, tap **Music** then toggle **Automatic Downloads** on.

Browse music that's stored on your device

Trying to listen to your music collection while in Airplane mode can be frustrating if most of your library is stored in the cloud. Thankfully there's an easy way to browse the music stored locally on your device. Just tap on the **Library** button then choose **Downloaded Music** and you'll see only music downloaded to your device.

Delete a track or album

Fed up with a song or album? Just **press firmly** on the track name or album artwork, then tap **Delete from Library** in the pop-up window.

Listen to Beats 1 Radio

Beats 1 plays the best music all day long, and it's presented by some of the most entertaining DJs in the world. To tune in at any moment tap the **Radio** button at the bottom of the screen. You'll see the Beats 1 station as the first result, so just tap on it to tune in. You can scroll downwards to see other stations and recently played music.

Listen to Beats 1 shows off the air

If you keep missing all the best bits of Beats 1 then don't worry! By following one of the DJs using Connect you can listen to recordings of their show as a playlist for later listening. To do this, open the **Music** app and search Apple Music for one of the Beats 1 DJs (such as Ebro Darden or Zane Lowe). Once you've found the DJ of choice, tap on their name, select **Connect** and you'll see their recent shows. You can listen to them individually, or follow the artist to automatically get the latest shows when ready.

See the top charts

What to see what's number one in the charts? Open the **Music** app, tap **Browse** then tap **Top Charts**. You can tap a song, album or video to start enjoying music, then sit back and relax as your device makes its way through the entire top charts.

Listen to your very own Apple-curated Playlist

Looking for some fresh beats to liven up your day? The Music app offers a playlist curated just to your tastes and it's automatically updated once a week with new tunes and beats. It's a clever feature and one that (hopefully) brings fresh music to your life. Here's how to find the playlist:

WEDNESDAY 18 APRIL

For You

New Music Mix

Updated Friday

1. Open the **Music** app and tap the **For You** button at the bottom of the screen.
2. Scroll through the playlists at the top of the screen until you find **My New Music Mix**.
3. You'll see a long list of tracks with a **subscribe** button at the top of the screen. Tap this and the playlist will be added to your collection – and updated automatically every week.

Like music to improve your recommendations list

Whenever you hear a great track or album, tap the options button in the corner of the screen (it looks like three dots) then tap the **Love** button. This tells Apple Music what genre of music you like. Keep doing this and over time the For You playlists and recommendations will get more and more accurate to your tastes in music.

Adjust your favorite artists in Apple Music

Is the music in the For You panel not quite to your taste? If so it's easy to tweak your favorited music genres and artists to (hopefully) show more accurate results. Here's how it works:

1. Open the **Music** app and tap **For You**.
2. Tap of your profile icon in the top left corner of the screen.
3. Scroll down then tap **View Account**.
4. Tap **Choose Artists For You** and follow the on-screen options for adjusting your favorite genres and artists.

Turn off Apple Music

If you'd like to turn off Apple Music and only see music purchased from the iTunes Store or synced to your device, then open the **Settings** app, select **Music** then un-toggle **Show Apple Music**.

Shuffle music

If you're bored of an album track order then tap the **Shuffle** button at the bottom of the screen to mix things up.

Watch TV & Films

Exclusive to Apple Music is a selection of TV shows, music videos and films. You'll find Planet of the Apps, which gives app creators the opportunity to pitch their ideas to entrepreneur advisors; and Carpool Karaoke, which features star-studded celebrity's sharing a car with each other.

If you're an Apple Music member then it's easy to watch Planet of the Apps and more on your iPhone:

1. Open the **Music** app.
2. Tap **Browse**, then choose **TV & Films.**
3. Find a show you like, tap on it then select an episode to immediately start watching.
4. To download a show, tap the small grey arrow next to the episode title then tap the **+Add** button.

If you're not a member of Apple Music, then you can still watch the first episode of each series, for free, via the iTunes Store app. Just open the app, search for the TV show name, then tap the **Get** button next to the first episode title.

Create a playlist

A playlist is simply a collection of music. It might be romantic music, tracks that go well while driving; anything you like. To create a new playlist of your own:

1. Tap the **Library** button at the bottom of the screen.
2. Select **Playlists** then tap the **New Playlist** button at the top of the screen
3. In the following panel you can add a title, songs from either your device or Apple Music, and even add a playlist album cover by tapping the camera icon in the thumbnail window.

Delete a playlist

To remove a playlist from your device, **tap firmly** on the playlist that you'd like to remove then choose **Delete from Library** in the pop-up window.

Only show music stored on your device

With Apple Music enabled you'll see every track and album saved to your device alongside the (potentially) thousands of tracks uploaded from your home computer. Such a large volume of music can get quite daunting, so if you'd like to only see the tracks and albums downloaded to your device, open the **Music** app, select **My Music** then tap the button below the **Recently Added** panel (it will likely say Artists or Playlists). Next, in the pop-up panel toggle **Show Music Available Offline**. This will only show music stored on your device.

Note, however, that toggling this option will prevent you from streaming tracks and albums from Apple Music.

Share your music

When you open the Music app for the first time, you'll be asked if you would like to share your music with friends and family. You can tap Get Started to set this feature up straight away, or if you'd like to do it later just tap the For You button, tap your user icon in the top-right corner then tap the Edit button below your name. Here's how it works:

1. Start by choosing a profile photo and user name.
2. Tap **Next**, then select if anyone can follow you and see your activity, or just those your approve.
3. Choose if you would like to show your custom playlists within your profile or in search on Apple Music.
4. Invite your friends to follow you on Apple Music. You can also connect to Facebook to add friends not in your contact book.
5. Tap **Next** and choose whether you would like to receive notifications when your friends start following you, when they add new playlists or when there's a new release or mix by one of your favorite artists.
6. Tap **Done** and you're ready to go.

Find and follow friends

If you know that your friends have similar taste in music to you, then it makes good sense to follow them on Apple Music, because by doing this you can see what they're listening too and what playlists they've shared. Here's how to find and add friends:

Follow friends

Connect Facebook   𝐟

SI Sam Ishan   INVITE

1. Open the **Music** app and tap **For You**.
2. Tap of your profile icon in the top left corner of the screen, then tap **View Profile** near the top of the screen.
3. Scroll down a little, then tap **Follow More Friends.**
4. Your device will scan your contacts book to find everyone who has Apple Music, then show them in a list.
5. Tap **Invite** to send them a friend request via the Message app, email or any social media apps you have installed.
6. You can also find people via the **For You** tab, which features friends that Apple Music recommends that you follow.
7. Finally, you can find people by searching for them. When you see a profile icon in the search results, tap on it to search that name.

Camera

In the world of mobile technology, 2007 was a long time ago. It was practically the stone age, a time when people pressed physical buttons to interact with their devices. Then one sunny January morning, Steve Jobs unveiled the iPhone.

You already know what an impact it made on the mobile industry — it revolutionized how we interacted with the internet and communicated with friends. The camera technology, however, was nothing new. The original iPhone had a 2-megapixel camera that could only take photos. It wasn't until the iPhone 3GS that the ability to record videos was introduced.

Over time, the camera app and hardware have become ever more advanced, until today it's able to recognize faces, analyze lighting conditions, record slow-motion video and much more. As a result, the iPhone in your pocket is capable of taking truly beautiful photos.

Snapping photos is done via the Camera app. It's a simple but efficient app that's packing some clever features, as this chapter will explain...

Take a photo

It's obvious, but to take a photo when the Camera app is open, just tap the **white circle** button at the bottom of the screen. After an image has been taken it will be stored within the Photos app. You can instantly jump the to saved image by tapping the small thumbnail icon in the bottom-right corner of the screen.

Take a photo from the lock screen

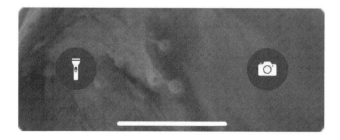

The quickest way to open the Camera app is via the lock screen of your iPhone. To do this, just press on the **Camera icon** in the lower-right corner. You can also swipe the lock screen towards the left, and the camera viewfinder will come into view.

Live Photos

Your photos represent treasured memories, stories and events from the past, but what if you could bring them to life for just a brief moment? Thanks to Live Photos this is now possible on iOS, and it's a magical feature that brings a smile to life, the crash of a wave into movement or a cheer into spontaneous eruption. Here's how it works:

When you take a photo your device automatically captures a few frames before and after the shot, as well as a brief snippet of sound. These aren't video captures, but raw, photo stills that look amazingly clear on the screen. To play a Live Photo back, just **press firmly** on the image when viewing it in the Photos app, and it will automatically play.

Turn Live Photos off

Live Photos take approximately twice the space of a regular photo. For most users that should never be an issue, but if you're running low on storage space, then you can switch off the Live Photo feature by simply tapping the yellow **Live Photo** icon at the top of the camera window before taking a photo.

Take a selfie

A selfie, named by Oxford Dictionaries as word of 2013, is simply a picture of oneself. To do this, you only need to swap to the front-facing camera, which is located above the screen. When using the Camera app, just tap the **swap camera** button in the top right corner of the screen.

The preview window will flip around and you'll see your own face on-screen. Tap the swap camera button again to return to the back-facing camera.

Take a photo with the volume buttons

You might not know this, but when using the **Camera** app it's possible to take a photo by pressing the volume up or down buttons on the side of your device. This is especially useful if it's bright outdoors and the screen is hard to see. It's also more satisfying to press a physical button than tapping a glass screen.

Use optical zoom to get a closer look

Want to take a photo of someone or something in the distance? Tap the **1x** button just above the camera controls, and the 56mm f/2.4 lens will activate, giving you a 2x view. You can zoom even further (up to 10x digitally) by holding your finger on the **1x** button then sliding it to the right.

Camera focus

The camera will automatically focus on a prominent object or area of light. Most of the time this is great, but if you need to manually focus the camera **tap on the area or subject** you wish to focus on.

Lock the camera focus and aperture

Sometimes the camera might struggle to focus on an area with lots of movement or lighting changes, or worse, it might continuously focus from one object to another. To lock the focus and aperture levels, **tap and hold** on a subject or area. After a second or two, a flashing yellow box beneath your finger will indicate that the camera focus has been locked. To unlock the focus tap again on the screen.

Swap camera modes

The Camera app has multiple modes, including Photo, Portrait, Video, Slow-Mo, Square and Pano. Each is explained further in this chapter, but to quickly jump to another mode, **swipe your finger either left or right** across the screen. You'll see the small text above the capture button swivel to the selected mode.

Take a portrait photo

Portrait photos are amazing. They mimic a DSLR camera by blurring the background behind a person. To do this your iPhone uses machine learning to automatically detect the face and hair of a subject, the distance between them and the background, then it blurs the background to create a beautiful 3D effect. You can also use this mode to create stunning photos of objects and nature, but it doesn't always work with 100% accuracy.

To use Portrait mode:

1. Open the **Camera** app and select **Portrait**.
2. Place the subject at least 2 feet away. If they are too close the Camera app will let you know.
3. Tap the capture button to take the photo.
4. Open the **Photos** app to see your portrait mode photo. Notice that a duplicate photo has been taken without the effect. Take time to compare them, then delete which ever you don't need.

Use Portrait Lighting mode to take amazing selfies

Our eyes are usually drawn to color, contrast, brightness and clarity. By focusing on these elements, you can manipulate images, tell stories and direct a viewers eye. In 2016, the iPhone 7 introduced Portrait Mode, which provided an amazing way to control the "clarity" of an image by focusing the camera on the person in an image, and not the background. In many ways it replicates a DSLR camera with a 50mm f/1.2 lens, making subjects 'pop' out of the background.

Getting the perfect portrait photo on iPhone can be tricky. Some backgrounds work better than others; you need to be stood a couple of feet away, and fuzzy hair can pose a problem. You'll beed to experiment a few times before you start to capture startling and beautiful photos.

Now, with iPhone XS, you can also capture Portrait Lighting photos. These are an extension to Portrait Mode, providing a handful of new effects that replicate a gold bounce card (Studio Light mode) and a black backdrop (Stage Light mode). They are:

Natural Light
Your subject's face in sharp focus against a blurred background.

Stage Light
Your subject's face spotlit against a deep black background.

Studio Light
A clean look with your subject's face brightly lit.

Stage Light Mono
Like Stage, but in classic black and white.

Contour Light
Dramatic shadows with highlights and lowlights.

Here's how Portrait Lighting works:

1. Open the **Camera** app and select **Portrait**.
2. You'll see five buttons appear towards the bottom of the screen: Natural Light, Studio Light, Contour Light, Stage Light and Stage Light Mono.
3. Select an effect by swiping through the options. Watch the screen to see the effect apply to your face in real-time.
4. Press the **capture** button to take a photo.
5. You can choose another effect, even after the photo has been saved, by tapping the Edit button within the Photos app.

Adjust the background blur of your Portrait Mode photos

One of the coolest new features of both iPhone XS and XS Max is the ability to adjust the background blur of Portrait Mode photos. No camera has had this feature before, so for a mobile phone to do it first is pretty impressive.

Technically, you're not physically adjust the background blur. Rather, the A12 Bionic chip within the iPhone is using machine learning to adjust the blur using software. Here's how it works: when you take a photo using Portrait Mode, the iPhone XS is doing a number of things in the background. First, it's using facial recognition to split apart the foreground from the background. Next, it creates a depth map using machine learning (basically, it's recognizing what's in the foreground, and what's in the background), then it progressively applies a blur effect between the two.

To adjust this background blur:

1. Take a Portrait Mode photo.
2. Open the photo using the Photos app.
3. Tap **Edit**.
4. Use the **Depth** slider to adjust the background blur. Slide it to the right to show less blur, or to the right to show more blur.

Disable the Portrait or Lighting Mode effect from a photo

If you take a Portrait Mode photo and don't like the result, you can turn off the blur effect by opening the image, tapping **Edit** then tapping the yellow **Portrait** button at the top of the screen.

Shoot a video

Capturing video is easy, just open the **Camera** app then swipe your finger across the preview window until the **Video** text is centered above the capture button. You'll notice that the capture button turns red. Tap this and the device will begin to record video. You'll see a white button in the bottom right corner of the screen. By tapping this you can take a photo while simultaneously recording video. To stop recording video, tap the **red record** button once again.

Enable 4K video recording

To enable 4K video recording, open the **Settings** app, tap **Camera** then select **Record Video**. On the following panel you'll be able to enable video recording at 4K by tapping the **4K at 60 fps** option.

Slow motion video

One of the most fun camera features included with iPhone is the ability to shoot video in slow motion. It works by filming 1080p video at 240 frames per second — that's up to four times faster than normal video. Once you've captured a clip it's possible to select a section and play it back at quarter speed for dramatic effect.

Film in slo-mo

While in the Camera app, swipe the text at the bottom of the screen until SLO-MO is centered. Next, tap the **red record** button to start filming your slow motion video. Keep filming, then tap the **red record** button again to stop shooting slow motion video. Your clip will now be saved in the Camera Roll. You can easily spot slow motion videos by the small ellipse shape made up of thin lines that appears on the thumbnail image.

Edit the playback speed

Tap on the video to open it. You'll notice a timeline at the top of the screen that's broken up by thin blue lines. In the center are two thicker black lines. These black lines determine which parts of the clip playback in slow motion. Drag them to the left or right to extend or shorten the slow-motion effect, then tap the blue **play** button at the bottom of the screen to see your edits playback.

Enable low-light video recording

A handy new feature for both iPhone XS and XS Max is the ability to slow down the frame rate in low-light condition. It works by lowering the frame rate from 30FPS to 24FPS when the iPhone detects low levels of light. This gives the camera sensor more time to absorb light, and vastly improves the image quality.

To turn this feature on, go to **Settings** > **Camera** > **Record Video**, then toggle **Auto Low Light FPS** on.

Burst mode

Action photos have always been hard to capture on mobile devices. Whether it's someone jumping mid-air, a vehicle racing by or a friend performing acrobatic moves, photos have previously come out blurry and mistimed. Not with the iPhone an iPad. They include a feature called Burst Mode, which works by taking 10 photos every second and then saves them into a collection in the Photos app. It automatically looks through all the photos you've captured, then picks what it thinks is the best one. It does this by analyzing the brightness, sharpness, whether there's a face in the photos and more. This is then saved as a Favorite image. You can of course, manually pick your own favorite with just a few taps of your finger.

Capture in burst mode

When you're ready to take a burst mode photo, **tap and hold the camera** button at the bottom of the screen. You'll see a counter appear above the button displaying how many individual images are being taken. When you've finished capturing in burst mode **let go** of the camera button. Note that you can also capture burst mode photos using the front-facing camera too, which is great for capturing that perfect group selfie.

Burst mode stacks

The burst mode images will now be saved as a stack in the Photos app. To see them, tap the **thumbnail** image in the bottom corner of the Camera app, or open the **Photos** app. You'll see the stack of images saved alongside any other photos you've taken.

Select a burst mode favorite

Open the stack of photos. To select a favorite, tap the **Favorites...** button at the bottom of the screen. A selection of thumbnails will appear. Scroll through them and tap on your favorite image. If you want to keep multiple images, just tap on them, each will be checked with a blue tick.

Tap the **Done** button to confirm your changes. A slide-up panel will ask if you'd like to only keep your favorite/s or keep everything. Tap whichever is relevant to your needs.

How to use the Camera timer

Setting a camera timer is a great way to snap a group shot, take a distant selfie or pose just the right way for a photo.

Open the **Camera** app and you'll see a timer icon at the very top of the screen. Tap it and you'll see three text options appear on-screen: Off, 3s and 10s. These correspond to the timer settings, so off is the standard setting, 3s gives you three seconds to pose, and 10s gives you 10 seconds to prepare yourself. Swipe your finger across the screen to select whichever is relevant to your needs, then tap the **Camera** button to snap a photo. You'll see a countdown appear on-screen and the camera flash will also emit a brief light for each passing second. After the countdown has ended your device will quickly capture 10 photos in a second. This stack of photos will be saved in the Photos app.

To pick a favorite, open the stack and tap the blue **Select...** text. Next, swipe through the images then tap the image (or images) you wish to save. Once you're happy with the selection, tap the **Done** button and the Photos app will ask if you'd like to keep your favorite image or all the images in the stack.

Capture time-lapse video

Have you ever wanted to capture a sunset, the changing tides or the movement of clouds? With an iPhone you can do this with the time-lapse feature. It works by capturing multiple photos, instead of video, over a long period of time.

To capture a time-lapse video, open the **Camera** app, then swipe from left-to-right until you see the TIME-LAPSE text appear on-screen. Next, place your device in a suitable location. Make sure it's steady – any movements over time will ruin the time-lapse effect. When you're ready, tap the **red record** button. Leave your device for a few moments or minutes - the longer the better as you'll capture more footage - then tap the **red record** button again to end the time-lapse.

Panoramic photos

Have you ever wanted to capture an incredibly beautiful vista? Maybe you're stood on the crest of a hill with a wide valley stretching out far below, perhaps you're trekking through mountains and want to capture the scene, or maybe the view in front of you looks particularly nice. Whatever the reason, with the standard camera view you're only going to capture a small piece of the vista. To get a wide, 180-degree image, you'll need to swap to Pano mode.

It works by taking one very wide continuous photo. As you rotate on the spot, the camera captures the image as it appears on the right side of the lens. This makes capturing movement of any kind nearly impossible, but for vistas and still scenes, it works wonders.

How to capture a panoramic shot

Begin by opening the **Camera** app. Next, swipe the text next to the Camera button until **Pano** is centered on-screen. The camera will now swap to Panorama mode. You'll see a thumbnail in the center of the screen with a white arrow pointing right. Tap the **Camera** button at the bottom of the screen to start capturing a panoramic shot, then slowly pan your device to the right.

Keep a steady hand — if you wobble too much black bars will appear at the top and bottom of the photo. Tap the **Camera** button at any time to end the shot, or keep panning until the preview thumbnail reaches the far right side. Once you've captured the image it will be saved to both iCloud and the Photos app. You can preview it on your device, but to see it at its full size you'll need to view the photo on a Mac or PC.

Camera filters

Filters enable you to instantly alter the appearance of a photo. There are eight to choose from: Mono, Tonal, Noir, Fade, Chrome, Process, Transfer and Instant. Each dramatically changes how your photos look, some with darkened shadows that add depth and drama, while others fade the color giving a vintage feel to your shots.

Filters can be great when used sparingly. Perhaps you're creating a poster for a themed party, or wish to emulate the look of a vintage camera. When overused, however, they can overwhelm the viewer and make images look unattractive.

Add a filter

From the main window of the Camera app, tap the **Filters** button in the bottom right corner of the screen. It looks like three overlapped circles. You'll instantly see all eight filters previewed on the screen. Tap on one and the filter will be applied to any photos you take.

Turn off filters

Tap the **Filters** button again to preview all eight. The middle option is called None. By tapping this you can turn off the filter effect and return to the camera preview panel.

Turn the flash on and off

The camera flash will automatically engage in low-light situations. This is handy some of the time, but there might be occasions where you don't need the flash, or don't want to startle others around you. To toggle the flash off, tap the **flash** button in the top corner of the screen. It's indicated by a bolt of lightning. You'll see options for setting the flash to auto mode, on or off.

Turn Smart HDR mode on or off

HDR photos are brilliant for capturing images in situations with both bright and dark areas. Maybe you're inside and there's a window with sunlight streaming through, or perhaps you're taking a photograph of friends standing in front of a bright sky. By default, HDR is set to auto mode. This lets the camera choose when to take a HDR photo. However, you can toggle HDR both on and off by going to **Settings** > **Camera**, then toggling **Smart HDR** off.

Enable the camera grid

Taking level photos can be tricky when only using the preview window, so to help line up horizons, trying enabling the camera grid. To do this, go to **Settings** > **Camera**, then toggle the **Grid** button on. Next, go back to the Camera app and you'll see a 3x3 grid above the preview window.

Preserve Camera Settings

Every time you close the Camera app, then re-open it, it defaults back to the Camera mode; no matter what you were doing before. If you want to use a specific mode, such as the video camera, swiping back to it can be a real pain.

Thankfully, there's an easy way to preserve the camera mode you were using last. Just go to **Settings** > **Camera** > **Preserve Settings** and toggle **Camera Mode** on.

Photos

The Photos app is a portal to your memories. Stored within its colorful icon are hundreds, if not thousands of treasured photos and videos. Photos of yapping dogs, family members, stunning landscapes, unflattering selfies and treasured holidays. This is one of those apps that you're going to be opening on a day-to-day basis, so keep it somewhere prominent on the Home screen where you can quickly tap it.

Open the app, and you'll discover a clean, tidy interface that appears to be basic and easy to use. In many ways it is, but dig a little deeper, and you'll find one of the most productive and in-depth apps available on iPhone. With just one fingertip it's possible to edit photos, create albums, move and delete images, view memories and much more..

Photos

Tap on the **Photos** button at the bottom of the screen and you'll see every photo ever taken using your iPhone. You can scroll through them using your finger, tap **Collections** in the upper-left corner of the screen to see groupings of photos, then tap **Years** to quickly scroll through thousands of images.

The Photos app instantly reads the location and time data within each photo and use them to sort the images. So if you're on holiday in San Francisco and take 10 photos by the Golden Gate Bridge, these will appear as a moment in the Photos app, titled Bay Bridge, San Francisco CA. During the rest of the holiday, you might snap another 100 photos, these will be organized as a collection, titled San Francisco, United States. Finally, all the images you take in one year will be titled 2013 - United States, Canada, England, etc.

For You

Next to the Photos button at the bottom of the screen is **For You**. This is one of the most powerful features of the Photos app. It works by organizing your images into events and albums, then presents these events in chronological order for you to enjoy.

Every day a new set of moments, people and categories will appear. You might see a memory of a day trip, a birthday, a family gathering, or even a "Best of 2018" album. Tap on one and you'll see more details about the moment, including the location and date. Some will also include a video, which includes beautiful music, editing and a tone that matches the subject matter.

Share an event

Whenever the For You section displays a new moment, it will offer the ability to share the corresponding photos with whoever is included in the moment, so if you go hiking with a buddy, the Photos app will let you share all the images with them in just a few steps. Here's how:

Keswick
17–20 Jun

Share with **Noah**?
77 Items

NEXT

1. Open the **Photos** app and tap **For You**.
2. Select one of the moments in the Sharing Suggestions field.
3. If someone you know appears in the photos, tap the blue **Next** button.
4. On the following panel, tap **Share in Messages** to send the photos to your friend.
5. You can also add additional people from your contacts list by tapping **+ Add People**.

Watch a video of an event

Whenever the Photos app suggests a moment, it will also offer the ability to watch is back as a video. To do this:

1. Open the **Photos** app and tap **For You**.
2. Select one of the moments which appears.
3. Tap the small blue **options** button in the top-right corner.
4. Select **Play Movie** from the pop-up field.

Edit and save a memory video

Memory videos are brilliant, evocative and subtle, but it's easy to customize each one to vary the duration or theme. Here's how it works:

1. Tap on a memory, begin playing the video then pause it.
2. Notice the options that appear above the scrub bar. They enable you to choose a theme and adjust the overall length of the video.
3. Tap on a theme (such as **Gentle** or **Happy**), then press **play** to see the changes made.
4. Similarly, tap on a new duration then press play to see the changes.
5. To save the video, tap the **Share** button in the bottom left corner then choose **Save Video**.

Shared

From the Share panel you can create shared albums for your friends and family to see – so long as those friends and family are also using iPhones or iPads.

Once an album has been created, photos and videos can be added, then contacts can be assigned who can see the images, like them and leave comments.

Albums

This section is pretty self-explanatory. It's where all your recently added photos can be seen alongside favorites, people, places, videos, slow-mos, time-lapses, burst photos, recently deleted images and more.

Search through your photos

The Photos app is incredibly intelligent. Using complex visual algorithms it can recognize objects, faces and places, then automatically organize groups of images into albums for you to enjoy. This clever form of visual recognition has another benefit: intelligent searching. You can access this search feature at any time while using the Photos app by tapping the Search icon at the top of the screen.

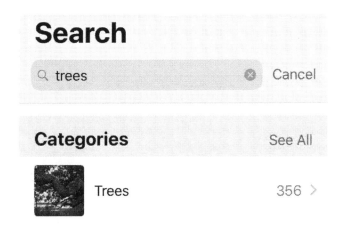

Search for *"California"* and you'll see all your photos of California. Search for *"Trees"* and you'll see (you guessed it) images of trees. You can be even more specific, however. So search for *"Trees in California"* and the Photos app will automatically show photos of trees within California. You can try other queries such as *"Tom eating pizza"*, or *"Sarah riding a horse"* and the app will instantly present you with the correct results.

People and Places

You might not know it, but your device intelligently scans every photo in your library to look for photos of locations and faces, then collates them in the People and Places section of the Photos app. To see these images just open the **Photos** app and go to **Albums** > **People & Places**.

Tap on the People thumbnail and you'll see shortcuts to everyone your device recognizes. Tap on the Places thumbnail, and you'll see a map view with all fo your photos overlaid, and placed in the correct location.

Watch a video

People albums include the ability to watch an edited movie, just like the Memories album. To see it just tap on a person in the People album then tap the play button near the top of the screen. Just like the Memories album, you can adjust the theme and duration of a video and save it to your device for later viewing.

Trim videos

So you've recorded an amazing video, but it's a bit too long. iPhone makes it easy to trim the beginning and end of any video to remove those unwanted or unnecessary moments. The resulting edit can be saved with just one tap, or saved as a new clip ensuring the original is left intact.

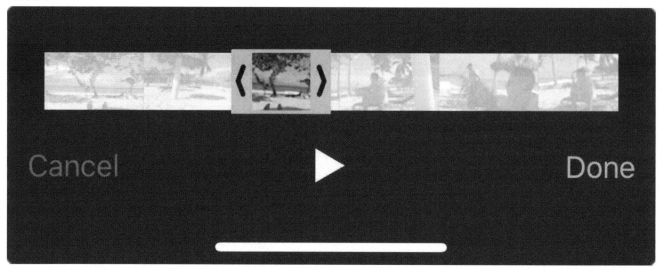

1. Either record a new video, or open one from the Photos app. You'll notice small black handles at both the beginning and end of the video, located at the top of the screen. Tap and hold one, then drag it to the left or right.
2. You'll notice that the grey handles have turned yellow, you can now use these to trim the beginning and end of the video. Drag the handles to eliminate any unnecessary content, then tap the **Trim** button at the top of the screen.
3. iPhone will ask if you would like to trim the original video, or create a new video with the edited length. Tap whichever is relevant to your needs.

Add a name to a person

While looking through the People album, tap on an individual's thumbnail to see all their photos. To add their name just tap the **+ Add Name** field at the top of the screen, start typing their name then select the relevant contact from your address book. If they're not saved as a contact don't worry, just tap the blue **Done** button on the keyboard and their name will still be saved.

Merge multiple photos

The Photos app doesn't always get it right – sometimes it might create multiple sets of photos for the same person. You can merge them into one collection by simply using the same name for both sets of images. To do this start typing their name, select their contact from your address book and the Photos app will ask if you'd like to merge the two sets of people.

Add someone to the Favorites area

If you like to regularly see the photos of a family member or friend, than adding them to the Favorites area of the People section is a good idea. To do this **tap and hold** on their thumbnail image until it "lifts" off the screen, then slide it to the Favorites area. Similarly, you can remove them from the Favorites area by tapping, holding and dragging them back down.

Add more people

Typically you'll see nine sets of thumbnails in the People area, but that doesn't mean there aren't more faces saved in your photo library. See the **Add People** button in the lower-right corner of the screen? Tap it and you'll see every person identified in your library. If like me, you have a photo library going back decades, then you're likely to be greeted with literately hundreds of smiling faces. You can add these collections to the main People library by simply tapping on them, then tapping **Done** at the bottom of the screen.

How to share a photo or video

Sharing photos is easy once you learn which icon to tap. Start by opening an image, then tap the **Share** icon in the bottom left corner of the screen – it looks like a blue box with an arrow pointing upwards.

A panel will now slide up the screen. From the top you can select more images to share, while the buttons further down enable you to send the photo/s via AirDrop, the Messages app, Mail app, iCloud, Twitter, Facebook and Flickr. At the bottom of the panel you'll see shortcuts for copying an image, creating a slideshow from it, assigning the photo to a contact, using it as a wallpaper or printing the image.

Select multiple images

Sometimes you might need to delete or share multiple images. To do this, make sure you're viewing multiple photos such as a collection or album, then tap the blue **Select** button in the right corner of the screen.

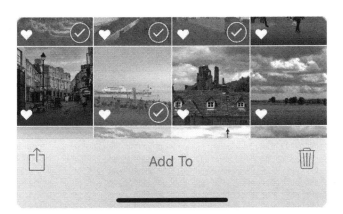

Next, tap on the photos you wish to select, or drag across the screen from one image to another. You can select as many as you like – there's no limit. Once you've selected every image you need to remove, tap the **trash** icon in the bottom right corner to delete them, or the **Share** button to send them onwards to friends and family.

How to delete a photo

While viewing an image tap the blue **Trash** icon in the bottom right corner of the screen. It's that simple.

See your photos on a map

It's not just an image that's taken every time you snap a photo on your iPhone. You probably didn't know, but a wealth of data is saved within the image. It's called the EXIF data. It's a lot of data, and it includes the GPS coordinates of the photo are recorded within the image, which means your iPhone can use these coordinates to show where a photo was taken on a map.

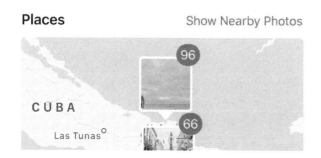

While viewing a collection of images, tap on the name of the location which appears above the photos then scroll down to see a map below the gallery and faces sections. Tap on the map, then zoom in using two fingers and you'll be able to see exactly where an image was snapped. This is a great way to re-live a trip by following your own footsteps.

Edit a photo

Want to improve the look of a photo you've taken on your iPhone? Begin by selecting an image in the Photos app, then tap the **Edit** button in the top right corner. You'll see the screen darken, and a number of editing tools appear. Turn over the page to find out more...

Automatically improve an image

Begin by selecting an image in the Photos app, then tap the **Edit** button in the top right corner. You'll see the screen darken, and a number of editing tools appear.

Begin by automatically improving the image. To do this simply tap the **Wand** icon in the top corner. This tool analyzes the image and changes its color, contrast and lighting to instantly make it appear more professional. However, if you don't like the change, just tap the **Wand** icon again to undo it.

Compare changes to a photo

If you'd like to compare your changes with the original photo at any time then tap and hold your finger on the thumbnail image above the editing controls. After a second you'll see the original image appear and (hopefully) prove that your edits have made a vast difference.

Crop an image

At the bottom of the screen are four icons. The first enables you to crop and rotate the image. Tap this icon, then either drag the edges of the image to crop it, or tap the small ratio button on the right to choose from a range of image ratio sizes.

Rotate a photo

While cropping a photo you can also rotate it in two ways. First, tap and **drag the rotate**

135

wheel below the image. As it rotates you'll see a grid appear that enables you to align straight edges or an horizon. Alternatively, tap the **rotate** icon to the left of the screen to instantly rotate the image by 90 degrees.

The middle icon at the bottom of the screen enables you to add a photo filter to your image. You'll find eight to choose from, each with its own unique appearance. Tap on each to preview it, or if you're happy with the original image just tap None.

Add a filter

Adjust the Light

The third icon at the bottom of the screen enables you to finely adjust the light and color of your image. Begin by tapping the Light button. You'll see a thumbnail bar appear with a red line running down it. To adjust the light, simply drag the bar with your finger, then watch the preview above to see the changes happen in real time.

To finely tune the exposure, highlights, shadows, brightness, contrast and black points, tap the small three-lined icon to the right of the screen, then select which element you'd like to change. You'll see a draggable bar appear at the bottom of the screen which enables you to finely tune that element.

Adjust the color

This feature works similarly to above, but enables you to adjust the color, saturation, contrast and cast of an image.

Bring a flat image to life

136

Photos taken using iPhone usually look amazing, but on occasion can look a little flat or overblown due to the small lens and sensor. Thankfully, the Photos app makes it easy to turn flat images into colorful, expressive shots. Here's how it's done:

1. **Start by editing a photo.** Select an image using the **Photos** app, tap **Edit** then tap the **Light** button at the bottom of the screen.
2. **Adjust the highlights.** Select **Light**, tap the **options** button (it looks like three dots with three lines) then select **Highlights**. Now pull the slider to the right using your finger and watch as colors and depth are revealed above.
3. **Adjust the shadows.** Either tap the **options** button again or scroll your finger upwards to choose **Shadows**, then drag the slider to the left and watch how as even more colors appear.
4. **Edit the brightness.** Swipe up or tap the **Options** button to choose **Brightness**, then drag the slider to the right by a small amount. Experiment with the other lights settings to see how they affect the image.
5. **Color Adjustments.** Let's adjust the colors of the photo. Begin by tapping the **Colors** button, then drag the slider left using your finger to subtlety boost the colors of the photo.
6. **Further adjustments.** Other tools you can experiment with include contrast and cast - the latter of which makes it easy to add warmth or coolness to an image. Feel free to experiment, with time you'll discover which tools work best with various scenarios and lighting conditions, and soon you'll be able to improve a photo in mere seconds.

Revert an image

If you ever want to revert an image to its original appearance, tap the **Edit** button then tap the red **Revert** text that appears at the bottom of the screen. The photo will now be reverted to its original state.

Edit Live Photos on iPhone

Live Photos are amazing. They're like the magical moving photos you might have seen in the Harry Potter movies, but they're *your* photos. Even if they seem a little cheesy now, in the distant future they'll become a wonderful way to relive moments from your past.

With the Photos app it's possible to edit Live Photos in exciting ways. For example, you can trim the video snippets before or after the photo, select a new keyframe, disable the audio or even change the visual effect animation of the Live photo. Read on to find out how...

Select a new key photo

If you've taken an action shot and noticed that the exact moment you wanted to capture is in the moving segment of the Live Photo then don't worry! You can easily edit the photo and select the exact frame as your key photo.

To do this open the Live Photo then tap the **Edit** button in the top-right corner of the screen. Next, using the scrubber, choose the frame you wish to set as the new key photo, then tap **Make Key Photo**. Once you're happy with your choice tap **Done** to save the new Key photo.

Trim your Live Photo

Sometimes you might want to trim a part of the Live Photo effect. Maybe you've captured someone doing something silly, or maybe you suddenly moved the camera at the very last second. Whatever the reason, it's easy to trim the beginning or end of the Live Photo effect.

To get started, select the Live Photo then tap the blue Edit button. Next, use the scrubber at the bottom of the screen to trim the Live Photo segment. To do this just slide either the left or right handle to fine tune the start or end points. Once you're happy with the results tap the Done button to save your changes.

Change the animation effect of your Live Photo

The photos app includes some amazing Live Photo effects that can be applied to your image:

Loop

This effect turns your Live Photo into a never-ending video loop. If you've ever seen GIF images on the web you'll know how this looks. It works best when the camera is perfectly still, or when there is little movement in the Live Photo.

Bounce

Bounce works in a similar way to the Loop effect, except instead of starting the Live Photo again, it plays in reverse once it reaches the end of the clip.

Long Exposure

This effect works by combining all the frames of your Live Photo into one image. For the best effect, hold your iPhone perfectly still then take a photo of moving object. Water looks ethereal and misty when viewed through the Long Exposure effect; while moving traffic blurs and streaks across the image.

To apply one of these new effects, simply open the Live Photo you wish to edit then slide the screen upwards with your finger. You'll see the Effects panel appear beneath. Just tap on the effect of choice to preview and use it.

Turn off the Live Photo sound

If you don't want to hear the background noise of your Live Photo then select the image of choice and tap the **Edit** button in the top-right corner. Next, tap the yellow **sound** button in the upper-left corner to mute (or unmute) the audio. Next, tap **Done** to save your change.

Revert your Live Photo

If you've made an unwanted change it's easy to revert back to the original Live Photo. Just tap the blue **Edit** button then tap the red **Revert** button at the bottom of the screen. After a second the Live Photo will instantly revert back to its original state.

Hide photos

If for any reason you'd like to hide a photo from the Photos, Memories and Shared albums, open the photo then tap the **Share** button at the bottom of the screen. Next tap **Hide** and confirm your decision.

Note that the photo is still available to see in the Albums view. It will also be copied to a new *Hidden* album where you can un-hide it if necessary.

Create an album

If you'd like to organize your photos and videos into albums then tap the Albums button at the bottom of the screen. If you've taken or synced any photos then you'll likely see a number of albums already present, including Videos, Burst Mode photos and Slo-mos.

To add an additional album, just tap the blue **plus** icon at the top of the screen. A pop-up window will appear asking for an album title. Enter one using the on-screen keyboard, then tap the **Save** button.

Next, we need to add some images to the new album. You'll see a window automatically appear which contains all the available photos on your device. Tap on as many images as you'd like, then tap the **Done** button at the top of the screen. These images will now be added to your new album.

Rename an album

While viewing the main Albums screen tap the **Edit** button. Existing albums such as Recently Added and Recently Delete can't be re-named, but any albums added by yourself can. Tap on the title of the album and the keyboard will slide up the screen. Update or change the album name, then tap the **Done** button when you're finished to confirm the changes.

Move an image from one album to another

Want to move an image from one album to another? **Tap and hold** on the image and you'll see a small black pop-up panel appear beneath your finger with the words Copy within. Tap the **Copy** text, then go to the album you wish to move the image too. Next, tap and hold your finger in an empty area of the album. You'll see another pop-up field appear beneath your finger, this time with the word Paste within. Tap **Paste** and the image will be placed within the album.

Delete an album

It's easy to delete albums from your device. From the main panel of the Albums screen, tap the **Edit** button in the top right corner of the screen. Small red buttons will appear alongside any albums you've created (note that you can't delete Recently Added, Panoramas, Videos or anything synced from a computer). Tap any of these small red buttons and the album will be deleted from your device. Keep in mind that any images contained within the album will still be stored on your device.

Create a shared album

By using shared albums, it's possible to share a selection of images with your friends and family. They can leave comments, like photos, and save them to their device.

Here's how it works: tap the **Shared** button at the bottom of the screen. If you haven't already created a shared album then tap the **New Shared Album** button in the middle of the screen. In the pop-up window, give the album a name (such as "*Holiday*"), then tap the **Next** button. On the following pane you can select contacts to share the album with. You can tap their name to enter a contact, or tap the plus icon and select contacts from the scrollable window.

Once you've added a bunch of friends and family, tap the **Create** button. The blank album will appear on-screen, to add photos and videos just tap the blue text that reads Add Photos or Videos.

Like a shared photo

While viewing a photo or video in a shared album, tap the Like button underneath the image to let all your friends know that you like the image. You can tap the face again to un-like an image.

Add a comment to a shared photo

While viewing a photo or video in a shared album, tap the **Add a comment...** field to leave a message for your friends to read. Be careful what you type, however, as comments cannot be deleted once shared!

Delete a shared album

While viewing the main Shared albums panel, tap the blue **Edit** button in the top right corner of the screen, then tap the small **red delete** button to remove the shared album. Keep in mind that the album will also be removed from your friends shared stream. This method of deleting albums in the Shared panel will also work with albums that friends have shared with you.

Files

If you've ever used a desktop computer or laptop, then you'll feel at home using the Files app. It's basically a Finder app for iOS, letting you organize, edit and delete files across all of your devices and cloud services.

Open the Files app and you'll see the Browse screen, with shortcuts to search through your files, browse iCloud Drive, see local files on your device and access any cloud-based services you have, such as Dropbox.

What you can do within the Files app

Files open or work in different ways depending on their file type. Some can be viewed and edited within Files, whereby others will open in their native app. To help you understand, here's a quick list of known file types and actions:

- Images can be previewed, edited and marked up from within the Files app.
- Video files can be previewed from within Files.
- Text-based files will open in their native app. If you don't have the correct app install then you can usually preview the file instead.
- GarageBand, Pages and Keynote files open in their respective apps.
- Zip files can be previewed, but you can't extract their contents.

Rename, duplicate, delete, share and tag files

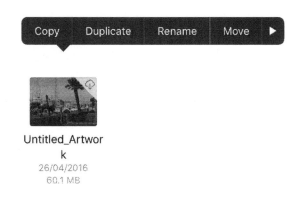

Untitled_Artwor
k
26/04/2016
60.1 MB

To quickly edit a file, tag it or share it, tap and hold until it lifts off the screen then let go. You'll see a small pop-up window appear about it, with shortcuts for all of the above.

Create a folder

Creating a new folder to organize your files is easy, just tap the **New Folder** button in the upper-left corner then give it a name in the pop-up window.

After you've created a folder you can drag a file into it by tapping and holding on any file until it lifts off the screen and attaches to your finger. Don't forget that you can multi-select by tapping on other files using another finger.

Move a file to another folder

If you'd like to move a file to another folder, here's what you need to do:

1. Tap the **Select** button at the top of the screen
2. Select the file/s that you want to move.
3. Tap the folder icon at the bottom of the screen, then choose the folder you want to move the files into.

Drag and drop

Poole Quay at Sunrise
26/04/2016
23.7 MB

Poole_Quay_at_ Sunset
29/03/2016
36.8 MB

Untitled_Artwork
26/04/2016
60.1 MB

One of the best features of the Files app is the ability to drag and drop files and folders. It makes organizing your files a breeze, lets you move multiple files and once and tag files using a swipe. To get started, **hold on a file** until it attaches to your finger. You can drag this file to another location, into a folder or slide it over a colored tag to add that tag.

You can also drag multiple files at once using multitouch. To do this, start dragging a file, then use one of your other fingers to tap on another file. You'll see it attach it to the stack under your finger.

If you add a file by accident there's no way to remove it from within the stack. If this happens your best option is to drag all the files under your finger to a tag. Sure, you'll need to untag them later, but it's less work than moving them all back using drag and drop.

Swap to List View

The Grid view is a great way to preview all

your files, but if you want to fit more things onto the screen simply tap the **List** view button in the upper-right corner of the screen.

Sort by size, date and name

While viewing a folder tap the **Sorted by Name** drop-down near the upper-center of the screen to sort your files by name, date, size or tag color.

Tag a file or folder with a color

Adding colored tags to files and folders is a great way to organize them or remind yourself of something that's important. To tag a file or folder, tap and hold on it until it lifts off the screen, let go then use the pop-up window to add a colored tag.

See file information

If you want to see information about a file, such as its modified date, size and file type, tap and hold on the file until it lifts off the screen, let go then tap **Info** in the pop-up window.

Maps

With a map of the entire globe in your pocket, it's no longer possible to get lost in a busy city or strange new land. That's exactly what the Maps app gives you, alongside directions, real-time traffic information, transit timetables, 3D views of major cities and more. All of this for free and accessible at any time. Let's take a detailed look at the Maps app to see how all of this is done...

Find a business or place

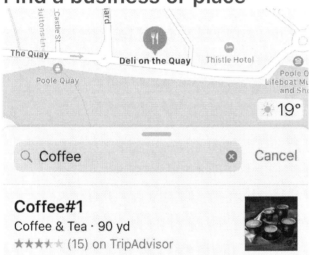

Looking for a coffee shop or the home of a friend? Just open the Maps app then enter a search term or address in the Search box in the lower half of the screen. You can try searching for *"coffee"*, or enter the post/zip code of an address.

You can also type the name of someone in your Contacts book to automatically load their address.

Helpful information

Notice the information listed below the search bar. This is generated using machine learning and your recent activity, so you might see how long it will take to get home, where your car is parked or where an event in your calendar is happening. Scroll down and you'll also see recent addresses, marked locations, and favorites. To minimize this information just pull the box down or tap the thin grey line above the search bar.

Toggle between display modes

The default Maps view is made up of vector graphics, which load incredibly quickly over a 3G or 4G connection, and look great to boot. However, if you'd rather see a satellite view then tap the **Info** button in the top-right corner then tap **Satellite**.

See a 3D map

Using the Maps app it's possible to navigate the world's most famous cities in beautiful 3D graphics. Buildings, landmarks, and even trees are modeled, enabling you to explore your way around a neighborhood like never before. Note that approximately 200 of the world's most popular cities have been mapped in 3D, so this mode only works with capitals and large cities. Nevertheless, it's an astonishing feature and fun to explore.

To view the 3D map, ensure you're in satellite mode (see step above) then zoom in on the map. To rotate the image, simply place two fingers on the screen then rotate them. To tilt the camera, simultaneously move two fingers up or down the screen. Moving them left or right will pan the camera.

Enjoy a flyover tour of a 3D city

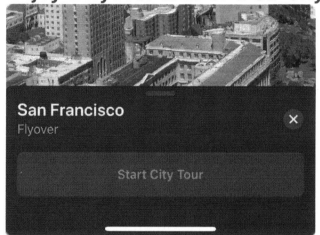

Want to explore a city like never before? Simply search for the city's name (such as San Francisco) then tap the **Flyover** button in the information panel at the bottom of the screen. You'll then be treated to a beautiful 3D tour of the city, stopping to see landmarks and interesting locations along the way.

Search indoor maps for airports and shopping centers

Airports and shopping centers can be massive, sprawling places with multiple floors and plenty of opportunities to get lost. With the Maps app you can find your way around using the indoor maps feature, which displays the locations of stores, toilets, transit stops, security desks and more.

Most international airports and major shopping centers are already mapped for you to explore. Simply look out for a "look inside" badge that appears beneath the name of the center, then zoom in to get a better look.

If there's something specific that you want to find, simply tap the **search** bar at the bottom of the screen to look for food stalls, stores, services and transportation links. If you're in landscape mode the search bar will be on the left.

If there are multiple floors to the building, you can navigate through them by tapping the number button on the right-side of the screen, just beneath the info and location buttons.

See photos and detailed descriptions of locations

After searching for a city or popular location swipe the information panel upwards to see photos, Wikipedia information and more about the location.

See Transit information

If you're exploring a location using public transport then it's a good idea to view the local area using the Transit view in Maps. This lets you see nearby train stations, tube lines, bus stations, taxi pick-up points and more. To enable this view simply tap the **Info** icon in the top-right corner of the screen then choose **Transit**. You'll now see subtle icons and shaded areas for selecting transit points on the map. Tap on one, then tap the relevant icon in the pop-up field and you'll see information for the next train/bus/tube, directions and more.

Rotate the map to match your view

If you're struggling to work out which way to go, double-tap the **arrow** button in the upper-right corner and the map will rotate to match whichever way you're facing. To return to the North facing view just tap the **compass** icon that has now appeared.

Drop a pin to find out more

To see detailed information about a specific point simply tap and hold your finger on the screen and a pin will be dropped underneath it. You'll then see the exact address for the pin, any shared photos, Wikipedia information, and also be able to add the address to your contact book.

Share a location

Want to send an address or place to friends and family? Just search for the location then tap the **Share** icon in the information panel at the bottom of the screen to send the current map view to friends and family.

Search Maps using Siri

If you'd rather search for a place or person using Siri, hold down the **Power** button until Siri appears, then say something like *"where is the nearest hotel"*, or *"how do I get to Starbucks"*.

Turn-by-turn navigation

Satellite navigation and GPS technology have made driving to unfamiliar locations so much easier; and with iPhone, you can take advantage of this same technology to explore and navigate the world. It's wonderfully easy to use. Once set up, Maps will display the route in 3D, with road signs, written directions, and spoken directions. And if the traffic conditions change, Maps will offer an alternative route for you to take.

To get started, open **Maps** then tap the **Search** field in the information panel. Next, enter the destination you wish the navigate too. This can be an address, zip code, or you can tap and hold on the map to drop a pin.

Once you've searched for an address tap the blue **Directions** button to enable turn-by-turn instructions. Maps will automatically find the optimal route to the destination. It will also offer alternative routes, if any are available, which appear as opaque blue lines on the map. You can tap on these alternative routes to choose them.

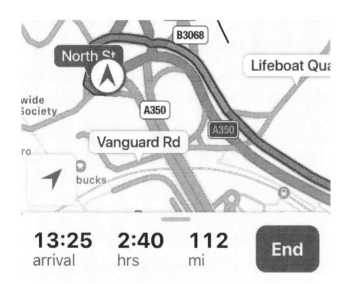

Once you've found a suitable route tap the green **GO** button to begin following turn-by-turn directions. The Map will zoom in and show your current location in the center of the screen.

Maps will automatically speak directions out-loud when you approach turns, lane changes, and roundabouts - just as you'd expect if using a dedicated Sat-Nav device. You can even press the **Power** button to turn off your iPhone display and it will light up whenever a change in direction is needed.

Find gas stations, restaurants and coffee shops along your way

If you need to take a break at any point during your journey drag the information panel upwards from the bottom of the screen then tap the relevant icon.

See an overview of your journey

You can see an overview of the journey at any time by dragging the information panel upwards then pressing the **Overview** button. This screen will detail the entire journey – which is helpful if you're taking a break from driving and need to plan the rest of the journey.

Mute or adjust the volume of the voice over commands

To turn off the Siri voice commands pull the information panel upwards from the bottom of the screen, tap the **Audio** button then select the relevant option.

How to get real-time traffic information

Planning a long journey and worried about the traffic? With the Maps app you can see live traffic conditions displayed on the map, with red-dotted lines that represent slow or stopped traffic, and orange-dotted lines that represent busy traffic.

To enable live traffic information, just tap the **Info** icon in the top-right corner of the screen, then toggle **Traffic** on.

How to report an issue with the map

The world is constantly changing, with new roads being opened, old ones being closed and buildings popping up everywhere; as a result the Maps app might not be 100% accurate in your area. To report an error or missing place, tap the **Info** button in the top-right corner of the screen then tap **Report an Issue**. On the following panes you'll be able to specify the problem, show it on the map then file a report.

News

We spend a lot of time reading news on the web. Maybe you get your news from traditional publications like the New York Times, perhaps you like to read blogs, or maybe you get your news from third-party apps. Now, with the News app on iPhone, all the stories you want to read can be found in one place.

That's because the News app collects all the stories and topics that you're interested in and presents them in one app. It combines the rich design found in traditional print with the interactivity of the web to create an immersive experience where the story comes to life like never before; and the more you read, the better News gets at understanding what topics you're interested in.

Add a News source or topic

Open the News app for the first time and you'll be greeted by the Get Started screen. From here you can add news sources by tapping on suggested favorites, and sign up for an email newsletter than sends you the best stories each day.

Once the app is set up and running it's just as easy to add and customize your news sources. To add a news source, tap the **Search** button at the bottom of the screen, enter a channel or topic name then tap the **plus** icon that appears next to it. To remove news sources tap the **Favorites** button, tap **Edit** at the top of the screen then tap the **delete** icon that appears over each channel or topic.

Search for topics and events

If there's a particular topic that you're interested in, tap the **Search** button at the bottom of the screen then type some keywords into the search field. The News app will search through thousands of channels and topics then show some recommended links. Tap on one to see more, or tap the plus icon to add the channel or topic to your Favorites section.

Save a story for later

Want to continue reading a story later? Tap the **bookmark** icon at the bottom of the screen and the article will be included in the Saved section of the News app. Now you can continue reading the story offline, or even on your other iOS devices.

Tell News what you like

or a much cheaper iPhone X remake would therefore support this theory.

       NEXT UP IN
                    TECHNOLOGY ▶

If you're reading a story and really like the subject matter or topic, tap the **heart** icon at the bottom of the screen.

This helps the News app to learn what subjects you like, so the more stories you heart, the more relevant the suggested news stories become.

Preview a story without reading it

Press **firmly** on a news story and you'll be able to preview it in a 3D Touch window before actually reading it. You can then press harder to "pop" into the story.

Show the menu and toolbar

If you're in the middle of reading a story and want to save, bookmark or share it, just tap the bottom of the screen and the menu/toolbar will slide back into view.

See your reading history

| Saved | History | | Clear |

HISTORY

◉ INDEPENDENT

Netflix considering buying cinemas to appease Oscar voters

50m ago

If you read a story recently and want to re-read or reference it, tap the **Saved** button from the homes creen of the News app, then tap the **History** tab at the top of the screen.

You'll now see your reading history stretching down the screen. To clear it, just tap the **Clear** button.

Health

The Health app is an entirely new way to view information and statistics about your health and fitness. The app can display a staggering amount of data in real-time, include heart rate, blood sugar levels, steps walked, calories burned, inhaler usage… the list goes on and on. This data can be entered manually, or automatically imported by devices on or around your body. For example, the app can wirelessly connect to the Apple Watch or Nike+ Fuelband and import steps taken and calories burned.

That's not all, because you can also create a medical ID card that's accessible from the Lock Screen, with details about any medical conditions, allergies, blood type and emergency contacts. This could help doctors and emergency workers to treat you more effectively in case of an accident.

As more and more health and fitness related devices are released, the Health app will become an essential tool that users are likely to check on a daily, if not hourly basis.

The Today tab

Open the Health app and you'll see the Today tab. From here you can view statistics about your health and fitness in real-time or see the last week, month or years worth of data.

The Health Data tab

Health Data

Q Search

Activity   Mindfulness

Tap the **Health Data** button at the bottom of the screen and you'll see a vast list of data types that can be tracked and monitored. At the top of the screen are four large shortcuts to Activity, Mindfulness, Nutrition, and Sleep. Tap any of these to see statistics about your recent activity, as well as shortcuts to recommended apps which might help you further improve your health and well being.

Add a Data Point entry

If you'd like to manually enter data and statistics, such as calories burned during exercise, then here's how it works:

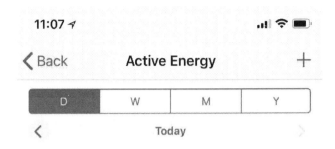

1. Select a data card, such as Active Energy.
2. Tap the **plus** button in the top corner.
3. Enter the relevant details, such as time and kcal.
4. Tap **Add**.
5. This method of adding data works across all data cards, so you can tell your iPhone how much sleep you've had, your blood pressure, plus much more.

Import steps taken from your iPhone

The iPhone includes a motion co-processor that automatically counts the steps you take throughout the day. This chip is always running in the background (don't worry it doesn't use up your battery life!) and saves the last seven days worth of data. This can be automatically imported into the Health app and displayed on the Dashboard. To add your steps taken, open the **Health** app and go to **Health Data > Fitness > Steps**, then toggle the **Show on Dashboard** switch. The Steps card will then be added to your Dashboard and show the last week's worth of data.

Create a Medical ID card

Having a Medial ID card set up on your iPhone is highly recommended. It can be accessed from the Lock Screen, giving emergency workers information about your health, allergies and medical conditions. To create your own Medical ID, open the **Health** app, tap the **Medical ID** button then tap **Create Medical ID**. On the following pane you can enter your name, age, height, medical conditions, allergies and reactions, medications, blood type, emergency contact and organ donor.

View a Medical ID card from the Lock Screen

In case of emergencies it's possible to view the Medical ID of a person from the Lock Screen of their iPhone. To do this press the **Power** button five times. This will activate the Emergency Lock screen. In the middle is a shortcut to the Medical ID card.

Home

The Home app is a little like glimpsing into the future. A future where all our home appliances are connected to the web, where it's possible to remotely open doors, adjust the temperature or change the lighting theme of a room – even when you're at work. For some, this future is already a reality, with smart homes being built across the globe. For the rest of us, smart lightbulbs and thermostats can already be bought in stores across the country, and they can all be controlled from the Home app.

After opening the app for the first time you'll see a home screen with a delightful plant-covered background. At the bottom of the screen are three buttons: Home, Rooms and Automation. Home is an overview of all your favorite devices, so if there's a light that you toggle regularly it will appear here. In the Rooms section, you can separate your devices into individual rooms. Rooms can also have scenes (such as night or day) to enable you to adjust multiple devices with just one tap. Finally, in the Automation section, you can set up your Apple TV or iPad as a hub, letting you control devices at home even when you're out.

Add a HomeKit accessory

You're going to need to add some accessories and devices to the Home app before you can do anything productive. Before you set up and add an accessory:

- Make sure it's powered on and nearby.
- Check your accessory's manual to see if it needs any additional hardware.

To add a HomeKit accessory:

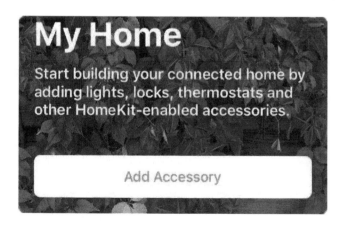

1. Open the **Home** app and tap either **Add Accessory** or the **plus** icon.
2. When your accessory appears, tap on it. If you're asked to Add Accessory to Network, select **Allow**.
3. Using the camera on your iPhone, scan the eight-digit HomeKit code or QR code. Alternatively, if you see a wireless icon on the accessory, you can simply hold your iPhone next to the device to add it.
4. Tap **Next**, then tap **Done**.

Customize the details of an accessory

Sometimes it's helpful to rename accessories or assign them to rooms. For example, if you have wireless lights in the kitchen then it's a good idea to assign them the *"Kitchen"* room.

To edit details for an accessory:

1. Tap the **Home** tab at the bottom of the screen.
2. **Touch and hold** on an accessory.
3. Tap **Details**, then edit the following:

- **Name**: Give your accessory a name to help you identify it.
- **Room**: Assign a room where your accessory is located.
- **Type**: Select the type of accessory it is.
- **Include in Favorites**: Toggle this on to access your accessory in Control Center, the Home tab, and on your Apple Watch.
- **Status and Notifications**: Tap this to see what accessories are turned on at the top of the Home tab, or to receive notifications for certain HomeKit accessories.
- **Group with other Accessories**: It's possible to group accessories together so you can treat them as one

Tap **Done** when you're ready to save your changes.

Add Rooms

It's a good idea to create Rooms in the Home app to help you organize your devices. To do this:

1. Tap the **Rooms** tab at the bottom of the screen.
2. Tap the **menu** icon in the top-left corner.
3. Tap **Room Settings**, then **Add Room**.
4. Give your room a name, such as Kitchen. To change the Room Wallpaper, tap **Take Photo** or **Choose from Existing**.
5. Tap **Save**.

To assign accessories to a room or zone:

1. **Touch and hold** on an accessory.
2. Tap **Details**, then select **Room**.
3. Select a room.
4. Tap **Done**.

Create a Zone of Rooms

Once you have a series of rooms created, then it's possible to create zones of rooms. For example, if you have two floors within your house, then you can assign the bedrooms and bathroom as Upstairs. Then you can ask Siri to do things like *"turn off all the lights upstairs"*. To create a zone:

1. Tap the **Rooms** tab at the bottom of the screen.
2. Tap the **menu** icon in the top-left corner, then tap **Room Settings**.
3. Tap on a room, such as Bedroom.
4. Tap **Zone**.
5. Tap **Create New**, then give your zone a name.
6. Tap **Done** to save the changes.

Create a scene to control multiple accessories

Scenes are where the Home app really comes into play. Think of a scene as a way to control multiple accessories at once. For example, when you arrive home you might want the garage door to open and all the ground floor lights to come on at once. To do this:

1. Tap the **Home** tab or **Rooms** tab.
2. Tap the **plus** icon, then choose **Add Scene**.
3. You can use the suggested scene, or create a custom one.
4. Tap **Add or Remove Accessories**.
5. Select the accessories that you want to add, then tap **Done**.
6. To adjust the settings for an accessory, just tap and hold on it.
7. To preview the scene, tap **Test This Scene**.
8. Tap **Done** when you're finished.

Invite others to control accessories

If you'd like others to control your home devices then it's easy to invite them using the Home app. Here's how it works:

1. Open the **Home** app and select the scene or accessory that you'd like to share.
2. Tap the **Edit** button in the top corner, then tap Invite...
3. Type the name of the person you'd like to invite, then tap **Send Invite** at the top of the screen.
4. Wait for them to join your connected home network.

Control Home devices from Control Center

Once you've added accessories to the Home app you can quickly toggle and adjust them via Control Center. It's remarkably simple to do, just swipe up from the bottom of the screen at any time then swipe to the right to see your music controls, then again to see your Home controls.

Use your iPad as a hub

If you have both an iPhone and iPad then it's possible to leave your iPad at home to act as a hub for all your Home accessories. That means it will take care of duties while you're out, adjusting the temperature, automatically turning on lights and more. To make this happen just connect your iPad to Wi-Fi and leave it plugged in. The device will do the rest of the work for you.

App Store

The iPhone is already a versatile device, with an amazing web browser, email client, great camera and more. But with a nearly endless supply of apps available within the App Store, you can do truly magical things with iPhone. You can interact with books in new ways, edit high-definition video and photos and even talk to loved ones face-to-face. Let's take a look at how you install and manage third-party apps on your device...

The App Store

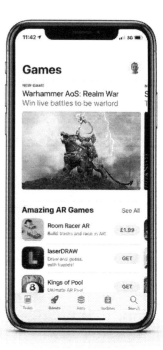

The App Store comes pre-installed on your device. Open it and you'll be presented with the days featured apps. You can use the Categories button at the top of the screen to browse app categories, and the buttons at the bottom to see featured apps, view the top charts, see Genius-recommended apps and search for apps by name.

How to install an app

So you've found an app that you like. How do you install it? It's simple, just tap the **FREE** button if it's a free app, or the price button if it's a paid app. After you've entered your Apple ID password, the app will be automatically downloaded to your device and you'll find it sitting on the Home Screen.

In-app purchases

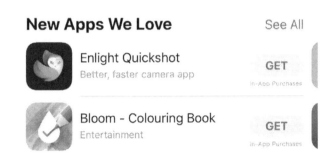

Wondering why that amazing-looking app is free? Chances are it has in-app purchases. If so, the text "In-App Purchases" will be displayed below the Get button.

Review an app

Want to tell others about how great (or terrible) an app is? While viewing it on the App Store, tap the **Reviews** tab button to see what everyone else thinks. Then, to leave your own review, tap the **Write A Review** button.

While writing a review you'll need to create a nickname, rate the app out of five stars and give the review a title. Keep the title short and descriptive, because the majority of visitors to the App Store only read review titles as they scroll through the page.

Note that you can only review apps that you've purchased and downloaded, and once a new version of the app is available your review will be moved to the All Versions tab.

Get support for an app

If you're having a problem with an app then you'll find support details within the App Store. To find it, locate the app in the App Store, then tap the **Reviews** tab button. Just below the Ratings and Reviews field, you'll see a blue piece of text called **App Support**. Tap this and you'll be taken to the support page for the app within Safari.

App updates

You'll be pleased to hear that apps automatically update on iPhone. However, if there's no wireless signal in your area, then all updates are kept in a queue within the App Store. You can see which apps are waiting to update, then update them manually if you please, by opening the App Store app then tapping the **Updates** button in the bottom right corner of the screen.

Turn off automatic app updates

Getting the latest version of an app is nearly always a great thing, because new features and optimizations often go a long way in improving the experience of an app. Nevertheless, there might be cases when you don't want apps to automatically update. Perhaps you've discovered the latest version of an app removes key features that you like? Or maybe you don't want to waste precious data bandwidth if you're on a pay as you go plan. Whatever the reason, it's a quick and easy process to turn off automatic app updates via the Settings app.

Go to **Settings** > **iTunes & App Store**, then under **Automatic Downloads**, toggle off the **Updates** switch. Apps will no longer update themselves.

Manually update an app

To manually update apps, you'll now need to open the **App Store** app, tap the **Updates** button at the bottom of the screen then tap the **Update** button alongside each app.

iTunes

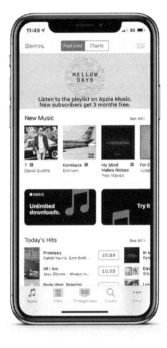

Want to download the latest music, TV shows and films? The iTunes app is the place to go. Since 2001 it has grown to be one of the largest entertainment retailers in the world, selling more than 25 billion songs worldwide. You'll find over 37 million songs to buy, 200,000 TV episodes and more than 50,000 films. Best of all, you can preview each song before you buy it, making the iTunes Store a great place to sample and listen to tracks.

However, for those who prefer to stream music, connect with artists and discover new tracks with ease, Apple Music — available via the Music app — is now the best way to listen to the latest tracks. For those who prefer to buy and own music outright, let's take a look at the iTunes app...

How to purchase download a song/TV show/movie

While viewing an item in the iTunes store you can purchase it by tapping the **price** button to the right of the track/album/TV show or film.

See the latest charts

Want to see who's number one at the moment? While viewing the Music/Films or TV sections, just tap the **Charts** button at the top of the screen. For music you'll see the charts split into top songs, albums and music videos, TV shows have separate charts for top episodes and series and film is just one big chart that you can scroll through.

Download new Ringtones and Alerts

The iPhone already comes with a vast array of ringtones to use, but if you'd like to use a song from contemporary music then open the **iTunes** app, tap the **More** button at the bottom of the screen then tap **Tones**. You'll discover an entire store filled with ringtones and alert tones from the latest albums, artists and music genres. Each is priced the same as a single music track but might only last for a few seconds, but they're a great way to add personality to your phone.

Discover new music and video using Genius

Finding a new album in the iTunes Store isn't exactly easy. Sure, you can browse the latest releases or see what's in the charts, but to find something that matches your personal taste and mood often takes luck more than skill. Thankfully, the Genius mode is here to help.

It works by examining your previous purchases and downloads to work out what you like, then suggests new songs, albums, TV shows and movies. To access Genius:

1. Open the **iTunes** app
2. Tap the **More** button and then select **Genius**.
3. You'll see a wide range of selections, with tabs for accessing Films and TV at the top of the screen.

Share an item

If you'd like to send an item from the iTunes store to yourself, friends or an app, tap the **Share** button at the top of the screen (it looks like a square with an arrow pointing upwards out of it) then select one of the share methods from the slide-up menu.

Redeem a gift card or promo code

iTunes promo codes make great birthday presents. They're also a handy way to let youngster buys apps, music and more from the iTunes Store without needing access to a credit card. If you've received an iTunes promo code and wish to redeem it:

Open the **iTunes** app, scroll down to the bottom of the page then tap the **Redeem** button.

After logging into your Apple ID account, the tap Use Camera button to take a photo of the promo code, or alternatively tap the manual button at the bottom of the screen to type the code yourself.

After the code has been verified its total amount will be added to your Apple ID account.

How to re-download existing purchases

It's easy to re-download an item from the iTunes Store at any time. Start by opening the **iTunes** app, then tap the **More** button at the bottom of the screen. You'll see a tabbed button called **Purchased**, tap it and you'll see every album, song, film and TV show that you've ever purchased. To re-download any of them, tap the iCloud icon to the right of each item.

Notes

On first glance, Notes app is a fairly basic way to jot down ideas and lists. It's much more than that, however. With the Notes app you can collaborate with friends, draw and annotate, scan documents, format text, create grids and more.

Create a new note

Open the Notes app for the very first time, and you'll see a blank canvas. To create and add your very first note, tap the **New** button in the top right corner of the screen.

Sketch a note

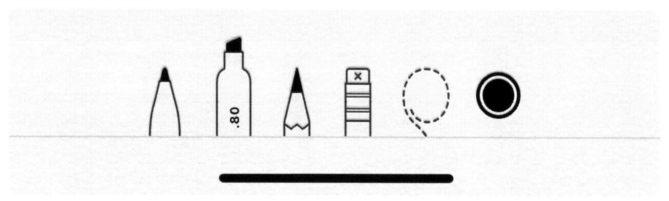

If you'd like to draw into a note, then tap the **plus** icon while editing, then tap the **pencil** button. A sketchpad will now appear on-screen, enabling you to draw with digital versions of a pen, felt tip or pencil. You can change the color of the line by tapping the small black circle.

Rotate a drawing

To rotate a drawing or sketch tap on it then tap the **Rotate Left** button in the top corner of the screen.

Delete a drawing

To quickly remove a sketch tap and hold on it then choose **Delete** from the pop-up field.

Create a checklist

To quickly create a checklist of items select multiple lines of text, tap the **plus** icon then tap the **tick** button. Each line will now be turned into a checklist of items. To mark a line as complete, finishing editing the note by tapping **Done** then tap on a checklist button.

See all your note attachments

If you'd like to quickly find a sketch or photo from all the notes on your device simply open the Notes app, select a folder (if necessary) then tap the **grid** icon in the bottom left corner. You'll now see every sketch and photo in chronological order.

Create a table

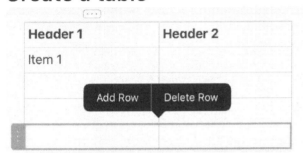

If you want to create a simple, beautiful grid, then start by creating or opening a note, tap where you want to insert the table then tap the **table** icon just above the keyboard. You'll see a 2-by-2 table appear within the note. You can add content to a row or column by tapping the appropriate area, or add additional rows and columns by tapping the buttons above or to the left of the table.

To copy, share, or delete a table, tap anywhere within the table itself, then tap the table icon above the keyboard. In the pop-up window simply choose the relevant option.

Insert a photo

If you'd like to add a photo to a note just tap the **plus** icon above the keyboard, select **Photo Libray** then choose the relevant image. You can also take a photo with the camera by tapping the plus icon then Take Photo or Video.

Share a note

Want to send a note to someone else? Just tap the **Share** button (it looks like a square with an arrow pointing out of it) and you'll see options for emailing the note, sending it to another device via AirDrop or copying it.

Collaborate on a note

If you'd like to share and collaborate a note with friends and family then it's an easy process on iPhone. If you're the creator of the note then it's yours to share, meaning you can invite others, see changes happen in real-time and remove anyone at any time. Here's how it works:

1. Select the note that you would like to share then tap the **Collaborate** button at the top of the screen (it's next to the Trash icon).
2. Use the **Share** panel to invite others from your Contacts book. You can send invites via Message, Mail, Twitter and more.
3. Anyone invited will receive an iCloud link to open your note. If they're using iOS then they can simply tap the link to open the note immediately.

4. As they make changes to the note you'll see them appear in real-time with a yellow highlight that fades away after a moment.
5. To remove someone's permission, tap the **Collaborate** button, tap the person's name then choose **Remove Access.**
6. To remove all access to the note simply tap the **Collaborate** button then tap **Stop Sharing**.

Print a note

While viewing a note, tap the **Share** button then select the **Print** option. iPhone can only print to wireless printers connected to the same Wi-Fi network, for example the HP Deskjet series.

Delete a note

Need to clear a note from your device? While viewing the notes list just **swipe across** the note you wish to remove from right to left. Alternatively, you can tap the **trash** icon while editing a note.

Search for a note

If you need to quickly find a specific note go to the home screen of the app, then pull down the notes list using your finger. You'll see a search field slide down from the top of the screen. Tap on it then enter the notes name, or alternatively a selection of text, and the Notes app will instantly search through all your notes.

Scan a document

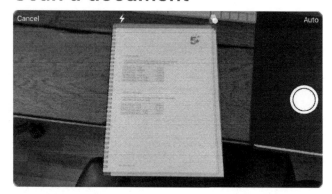

Using the notes app, it's possible to scan letters and documents, then attach them directly to a note. What's great is that scans actually look like scanned documents, thanks to some clever post-processing which straightens the image and fixes any white balance issues. Admittedly the sharpness isn't as good as a real scan, but it's good enough for more uses.

To scan a document:

1. Open an existing note or create a new one
2. Tap the **plus** icon above the keyboard
3. Select the **Scan Documents** option
4. When the camera view appears, move it over the document you wish to scan and your iPhone will automatically recognize it and place a yellow box over the top
5. Tap the **shutter** button to capture the document
6. If needed, you can adjust the corners of the scan using your finger
7. Once you're happy with the scan, tap **Keep Scan** to save the image.

Edit a scanned document

Once you've captured a document scan with your iPhone, you can adjust it's color, rotate the scan or use Markup to add notes and sketches. To get started tap on a scanned document to bring up the editing toolbar. You'll see shortcut buttons to adjust the crop, convert the scan to Greyscale, Black and White or Color; or rotate the scan by 90 degrees.

Turn off a Notes account

If you don't need multiple Notes accounts then go to **Settings** > **Passwords & Accounts**. On the following screen you'll see a list of all your accounts. Tap the account you wish to remove from the Notes app then de-toggle the Notes switch.

Change the default Notes account

The default notes account is used whenever you create a new note. If for any reason you need to change it, go to **Settings** > **Notes**, then tap the **Default Account** option.

Clock

The Clock app is a handy shortcut to setting alarms, timers, seeing world clocks and enabling Bedtime – a handy way to get a good night's sleep. On first appearances, it's a simple app, but dig a little deeper and some great features can be discovered.

Set an alarm

By tapping the **Alarm** button at the bottom of the screen you can add and edit alarms for any time of the day. Here's how it works:

1. Tap **Add** in the top-right corner then use the scrollers to pick an hour and minute.
2. Tap **Repeat** to choose what days the alarm goes off.
3. Select **Label** to give your alarm a unique name (helpful if you're using an alarm as a reminder)
4. Pick a sound or song by tapping the **Sound** button
5. Toggle **Snooze** on or off if you think you'll need some extra time after the alarm has begun.

Use Bedtime to get a good night's sleep

Use it properly and Bedtime might become your favorite feature about the Clock app. It's essentially a smart alarm clock. One that nudges you to go to bed at the right time, then in the morning gently awakens you with soothing music. But it's much cleverer than just that. The app works out when you actually wake up (by monitoring when you pick up your phone), can learn your sleeping patterns over time and uses clever volume control and vibration patterns to subtly wake you up. Here's how it works:

1. First of all, open the **Clock** app and tap **Bedtime**.
2. Next, tell Bedtime what time you would like to wake up. This will help the app work out how much sleep you need to feel refreshed at the right time.
3. Set the days of the week for when you would like the alarm to go off. For most of us it's probably Monday to Friday.
4. Tell Bedtime how many hours of sleep you need. Most adults need between 7 and 8 hours.
5. Tell the app when you would like to be reminded to go to bed. 30-minutes is usually a good amount of time.
6. Pick an alarm. There are nine music tracks to choose from, all of which are – thankfully – soothing and calm. Never again will you be jolted out of sleep by a screaming alarm.
7. Stay consistent. You'll be reminded to try and keep your sleep patterns consistent throughout the week. Bedtime does this by showing you a Sleep History chart – the closer the vertical lines are aligned the better your sleep patterns.
8. Tap **Save** and you'll see a gold doughnut chart of your sleep times.

Adjust Bedtime Settings

If you'd like to change your alarm, reminder duration, volume or days of the week when Bedtime is in use then open the **Clock** app, tap **Bedtime** then tap **Options** in the top-left corner of the screen. You can also drag the gold doughnut chart wheel with your finger to make fine adjustments to your sleep times.

Use the Stopwatch

Tap the **Stopwatch** button and you'll see a basic Stopwatch for setting times and laps. It works exactly how you might imagine; just tap the green **Start** button to begin, tap the **Lap** button to record a lap and tap **Stop** to pause the Stopwatch. You can then reset the stopwatch or check out your lap times at the bottom of the screen.

Set a timer

Whether you're cooking an egg, timing a sporting event or setting a reminder, using the timer function is a handy way to keep track of time. It's easy to use, just tap the **Timer** button at the bottom of the screen, use the scrollers to set the hours and minutes then tap **Start**. You can also change the timer alert sound by tapping **When Timer Ends** then choosing an effect from the list.

Weather

If you live a considerable distance away from the equator, then chances are the local weather changes from day-to-day.

The weather has become a national obsession in countries such as the United Kingdom, where snow might give way to sizzling heat over the course of just a few days. As a result, the Weather app is often one of the most apps on iPhone and is nearly always sitting on the first home screen of iPhones around the world. It's a basic app, pulling in local weather reports and predicting the week ahead, but it's also possible to see whether from thousands of cities around the world...

See a detailed overview

Open the Weather app and you'll see a simple overview of the current conditions, with icons and temperatures for the hours and days ahead. However, it's possible to see a more detailed panel that includes sunrise/set times, the chance of rain, wind direction, precipitation, pressure, visibility and UV index. To see this panel, simply drag the screen upwards. You'll then see the detailed weather panel slide into view.

Swap between Fahrenheit and Celsius

By default, the Weather app displays temperatures in Fahrenheit, but you can easily swap it to Celsius by tapping the **menu** button in the bottom right corner, then tapping either **°C** for Celsius or **°F** for Fahrenheit.

See the weather in another city

If you're travelling to another city and want to see it's weather forecast, then tap the **menu** button in the bottom right corner of the screen. You'll see a list of cities appear, each with a graphical overview of the current conditions. Tap on one to see an overview of the week ahead, or tap the **plus** button to search and add another city.

Stocks

Whether you're keeping an eye on the latest stocks, betting against them, or monitoring your portfolio, the Stocks app in iOS 12 has received a massive overhaul which improves its usefulness and overall experience.

The basics

Open the Stocks app, and the first thing you see is an overview of the leading 5 stocks or markets, with the latest news stories at the bottom of the screen.

To add a new stock, tap on the **Search** field near the top of the screen, and search for either the company name or its stock name. Once you've found it, tap the green **plus** button to add it.

Digging a bit deeper

Here are some of the other things you can do within the Stocks app to dig a little deeper into stock results and news:

- Tap on an individual stock and you'll see a graph of its latest performance. If it's colored green, then the stock is generally doing well. If it's red, then (you guessed it) it's not performing that well.
- If you place your finger over a point on the share graph, you'll see the exact figure it was on that day and time:

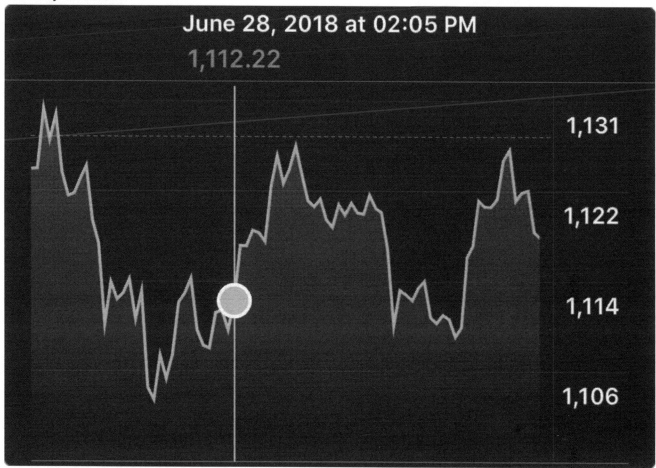

- Scroll down and you'll see news for that particular stock, tap on one and you can read the full story.
- To go back to the main Stocks window, pull the individual stock view down from the top of the screen.
- To rearrange the Stocks on the home panel of the app, tap the small **options** button in the bottom-right corner of the screen, then drag the stocks up or down using the sort buttons on the right. From the options panel you can also delete stocks by tapping the red **delete** buttons.

Compass

Not only can your iPhone display the true direction of North, East, South and West, but it also has an inbuilt level meter, making it easy to work out the angle of tables or even hang a perfectly straight picture on the wall.

Follow a bearing

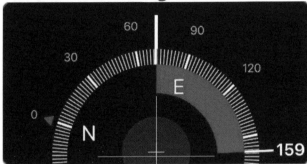

If you want to follow a particular direction (for example straight East) then open the Compass app, calibrate it if necessary, then tap once in the middle of the compass. You'll see the current direction marked with a number, and as you move around the compass will draw a red line on the inside of the circle to show how far you've deviated from the original bearing.

Swap between magnetic North and true North

By default, the iPhone measures the magnetic North (the point at which the planet's magnetic field points vertically downwards). To see the true North, in which the device points towards the North Pole, go to **Settings** > **Compass** and toggle **True North** on.

Measure

Every so often, an app comes along and replaces a common everyday tool. Since the iPhone's launch in 2007, we've seen apps replace the pocket camera, a torch, a compass... the list goes on and on; and now, with the release of iOS 12, we're getting a replacement for the measuring tape.

You should see the new Measure app on the Home screen on your iPhone. If you don't see it, pull down the screen then search for *"Measure"*.

Open the app, and you'll notice a simple interface. There's a button for adding a start and end point for the measuring "tape", a camera button for taking photos, a back button, to undo any mistakes you make, a clear button for starting again, and a Level button, which replaces the level tool which used to be in the Compass app.

Measure a straight line

When you're ready to measure something, point your device at it, line the dot with the start point, then tap the large **plus** button. Now, move your device to start measuring, and when you get to the end point, tap the **plus** button again to complete the measurement. Notice that if you step back, the measurement line stays aligned with the real-life object, and that if you turn around then come back, the measurement is still there. Clever!

Measure an object

If you would like to measure an object, such as a painting or cupboard, then here's what to do:

1. Align the centre dot with a corner of the object. If your device recognizes the corner you'll feel a subtle bump.
2. Tap the **plus** button to mark the first measurement point.
3. Move your device to the second point, then tap the **plus** button to mark it.
4. Next, align the centre dot with the second point you just marked, and tap the plus button. If you aligned it properly, then the measurement points will be linked together.
5. Continue making measurement points, until you've captured the whole object. You can now see all of its measurements on the screen.

Copy a measurement

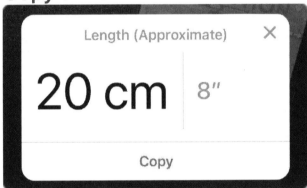

Whenever you measure something, tap on the measurement to display a pop-up window with all of its details. From this window, you can also copy the measurement, then paste it into another app.

Use the level tool

Look at the bottom of the screen when using the Measure app and you'll notice a **Level** button. Tap this, and the screen will display a levelling tool, which you can use to accurately work out the angle of an object, such as a table surface. When the object is entirely level, you'll see the lower half of the screen turn green.

Reminders

The iPhone already includes a notes app that can be used to jot down ideas and thoughts, but Reminders makes it easy to create to-do lists, set deadlines and organize your life. It can also remind you with alerts at pre-determined times.

That's not all the app does, of course. It can group reminders into categories and even automatically sync reminders across all your devices via iCloud.

Create a new Reminder

Open the **Reminders** app and you'll see a blank set of reminder cards in the center of the screen. Tap the **New List** reminder to create a new list. Give the list a name, you can also specify its color by tapping on a colored dot. Once you're happy and ready to start entering items, tap the **Done** button.

Reminder items

While viewing a list, tap on an item and you'll see a small info icon appear on its right side. Tap this and you'll see options for editing the items name, setting a reminder, assigning its priority and the ability to add notes.

Mark a Reminder as complete

While viewing reminders, you can mark them as complete by tapping the small **circles** next to each entry.

How to close a reminder list

While viewing a reminders list you'll see a small set of cards at the bottom of the screen. Tap these to go back to the main Reminders window.

How to rearrange reminder lists

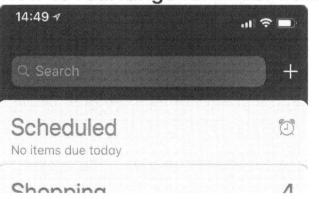

To move reminders lists around, simply tap and hold on a reminder until it slides up beneath your finger, then move it to another position.

Schedule items

Any reminders added to the Scheduled field will automatically include an alert that triggers on a set date or time. To configure the alarm details, tap on the **time** or **i** icon to the right of the notification. From the pop-up window you can set the alarm time and repeat settings.

Delete Reminders

Tap the **Edit** button while viewing a reminder to delete it or rearrange its items. To delete items, tap the red **circle** that appears alongside each reminder. To rearrange them, just tap and drag the **sort** button to the right of each reminder.

Create a Reminder using Siri

You can also add reminders by using Siri. Just tap and hold the **Power** button, then say something like *"Remind me to pick up Sam"*. Siri will then automatically create a new reminder for you.

Settings

Open the Settings app and you'll find a wealth of options for customizing your iPhone. It's possible to configure Notification Center, add security features, change screen settings and much more. The Settings app is also an important tool for enabling accessibility tools.

General Settings

Whenever you want to make a change to your iPhone, adjust a setting or update the system, then the Settings app is the place to go.

Open the Settings app and you'll see a list of shortcuts to all the important settings on your iPhone. They're labelled logically, so if you want to adjust how apps notify you, then tap on the Notifications shortcut. Similarly, if you want to connect to a new Wi-Fi network, tap Wi-Fi.

Search through Settings

Settings

Q Search

The Settings app is packed with toggle switches, fields and features for customizing how your iPhone works. Many are hidden away in sub-sections that you probably wouldn't find unless you were really determined, so if you need to quickly change a setting open the Settings app and drag the screen down. A search bar will appear, enabling you to quickly find a setting or switch.

Find individual app settings

Nearly all the apps installed on your iPhone have their own settings. Usually, you can turn off location awareness, push notifications or background app refresh. Sometimes you'll see specific settings, like the ability to upload HD photos and videos to Facebook.

To access these app settings, just open the **Settings** app then scroll down. Keep going, and eventually you'll find all the individual app settings on your device. You can also search for an app name by using the search box at the top of the Settings window.

See battery usage per app

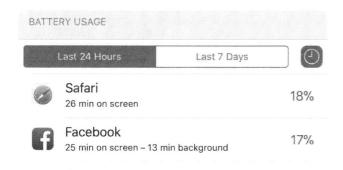

If you're worried that an app is responsible for draining the battery life on your iPhone, go to **Settings** > **Battery** and scroll down a little. From **Battery Usage** panel you'll see a breakdown of the battery usage over the last 24 hours and/or seven days. To see exactly how much time you've spent within each app, tap the **clock** icon and you'll see its usage in minutes.

Enable Low Power mode

If you've had a long day and you're iPhone is running out of battery life, it's possible to enable Low Power mode, which turns off background processes and certain animations to add approximately one extra hour of battery. To enable this feature go to **Settings** > **Battery**, then toggle **Low Power Mode** on.

Use 3D Touch to quickly access areas

From the Home screen, you can press firmly on the **Settings** app icon and you can quickly access settings for Bluetooth, Wi-Fi, Mobile Data and Battery.

Choose a new wallpaper

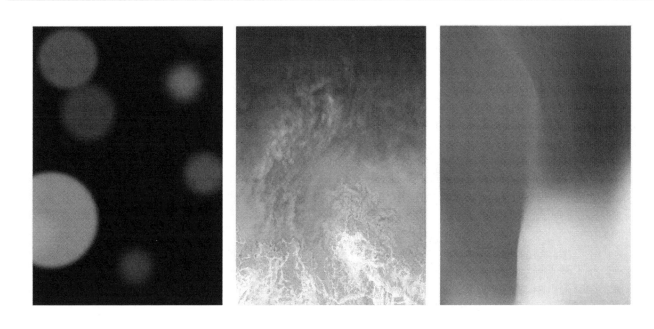

Changing the background wallpaper is always a great way to freshen the look and feel of your iPhone. It's easy to do, just open the **Settings** app, tap **Wallpaper** then **Choose a New Wallpaper**. On the following screen you can pick between a number of still, live and dynamic wallpapers. You can also browse your photo library to choose one of your own images.

Turn off System Haptics

Every now and then your iPhone will make a subtle vibration to let you know something has happened. When you scroll through drop-down lists you can feel each field as it scrolls by. When you take a photo there's a subtle click, and when you use 3D Touch you can feel a "pop" beneath your finger.

If you don't like these effects, you can disable them by going to **Settings** > **Sounds & Haptics**, then toggling **System Haptics** off.

Screen Time

If you're concerned or worried that you might be spending too long using your device, then the Screen Time panel included in the Settings app will help you work out exactly how long you've spent using apps, how many notifications you've received, or set time limits to prevent future distractions. Here's an overview of how it works:

Find Screen Time

1. Open the **Settings** app.
2. Tap on **Screen Time**.
3. Tap your device at the top of the panel.
4. You can then view your Screen Time data for the current day or the last 7 days.

As you'll see, the Screen Time panel is dense with information. You'll see total time spent with apps (some will be grouped into categories, such as "Productivity", how many times you've picked up your device, and how many notifications you've received. If you choose to view data for the last 7 days then you'll get a broader picture of how you use your device.

Create an activity report

Using the Screen Time panel it's possible to create weekly reports to see app usage, notifications, and device pickups. Here's how:

1. Open the **Settings** app, then tap on **Screen Time**.
2. At the top of the panel you should see a brief report on your devices use. If not, tap on **All Devices**, then choose the **Last 7 Days** tab.
3. From here you will see a brief overview of the total time spent on your device, broken down into categories.
4. Beneath is a panel that displays which apps you've used the most. Tap on one, and you'll see a bar chart of the total time spent over the course of a day or week.
5. Below the Most Used panel is the Pickups panel, this displays exactly how many times you've picked up your device, as well as the average amount of time passed between pickups.
6. At the bottom of the activity report panel is the total number of notifications you've received. It's broken down by app, so you can see exactly which app is sending your the most notifications.

Set an app limit

If you're worried that you're spending too much time using specific apps and websites, then you can set time limits to prevent over usage.

  ## Reading & Reference
Reading & Reference

  ## Games
Games

1. Open the **Settings** app, then tap on **Screen Time**.
2. Tap on **App Limits**, then choose A**dd Limit**.
3. By default, all apps and categories are selected, but you can choose a specific category for tapping on it, such as Games, or Entertainment.
4. Tap **Add**, then set a time limit using the hours and mins sliders.
5. To limit apps depending on the day, tap **Customize Days**, tap on a day, then set a limit.
6. You can enable a 5-minute warning, by toggling **Ask for More Time**.

Block inappropriate content

If you would like to limit inappropriate content, such as explicit music, R-rated films, or adult websites, then here's how:

1. Open the **Settings** app, then tap on **Screen Time**.
2. Tap on **Content & Privacy**, then choose **Content Restrictions**.
3. Tap on a subject matter, such as **Films**, then select an option. For example, in Films you can limit movie playback to U, PG, 12, 15, or unrated.

Other things you can restrict using Screen Time

By visiting the **Content & Privacy** panel in the Screen Time settings, you can limit a massive amount of content and features on a device, including:

- App installation
- Location Sharing
- Changes to passcodes
- Account changes
- Mobile data limits
- Volume limit
- Explicit language
- Screen recording
- Multiplayer games

Set a downtime

Using the Screen Time settings panel it's possible to limit apps and notifications at a specific time, such as bedtime. To do this:

1. Open the **Settings** app, then tap on **Screen Time**.
2. Tap **Downtime**, then enter your pin.
3. Toggle **Downtime** on, then use the **Start** and **End** buttons to set a schedule.
4. You can enable a 5-minute warning, by toggling **Ask for More Time**.

Battery Settings

You might not know it, but batteries don't last forever. That's because every time you re-charge your iPhone, a tiny fraction of its battery capacity is lost. This means that if you re-charge your device every night, after a year it might lose approximately 10% of its original capacity.

The latest iPhone's do a pretty good at alleviating this problem thanks to some clever battery management techniques, but nevertheless, over time they will degrade to a small extend. Here's how you can see how your battery us faring, and what to do if it has degraded more than you were expecting...

See the total capacity

Let's start by checking the battery's current capacity. To do this:

1. Open the **Settings** app.
2. Tap on **Battery**.
3. Select **Battery Health.**
4. On the following screen you'll see its maximum capacity, relative to how it was when you first purchased the device.

Battery Performance Management

If the battery has lost some of its original capacity, then Performance Management mode will be enabled and you will see this message:

This iPhone has experienced an unexpected shutdown because the battery was unable to deliver the necessary peak power. Performance management has been applied to help prevent this from happening again.

Performance Management works by throttling the CPU of your device to prevent it from shutting down unexpectedly. This can sometimes happen when you do a CPU-intensive task (such as gaming). To turn this off, tap the **Disable** button.

Please note that if you disable performance management, you can't turn it back on. Instead, it will be turned on again automatically if an unexpected shutdown occurs. The option to disable it will then reappear.

If the total capacity is less than 80%

Chances are you've had your device a long time. Either that or you've re-charged it many many times. You're best option is to get the battery replaced by Apple. You can do this by sending it in for repair, by making an appointment at an Apple Store, or by visiting an authorized Apple Service Location.

To schedule a collection of your device, or to make an appointment with your local Apple Store, visit this URL: goo.gl/C4bHS1 It will take you Apple's website where you can select your device and arrange for the battery swap.

Battery Replacement Pricing

If your iPhone is still within its warranty, or you have AppleCare+ cover, then the price of a replacement battery is free, otherwise, it's $29.

See your battery level over the last day

If you're worried that an app or service is using all your battery, then you can access a time chart which displays the battery level and activity over the last 24 hours, or 8 days. To do this:

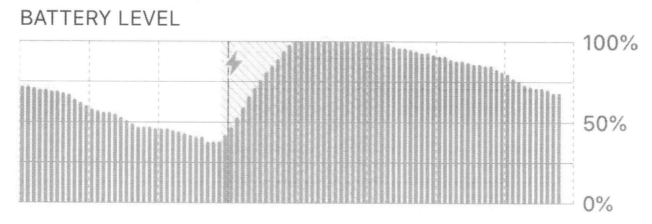

1. Go to **Settings** > **Battery**.
2. Scroll down and you'll find two charts covering your batteries charge level and activity.
3. You can toggle between the last 24 hours and 8 days using the blue tab above the charts.
4. Scroll down and you'll see a breakdown of which apps used the most battery. Tap on one and you'll see the exact amount of time each app was used, and for how long it has been running in the background.

Enable Low Power Mode

If you'd like to extend your devices battery for as long as possible, then iOS offers a handy mode whereby background activity, such as downloads and mail fetch, are switched off. The screen brightness is also reduced, and push notifications are checked more often. To enable Low Power Mode, go to **Settings** > **Battery**, then toggle **Low Power Mode** on. You can also enable and disable it from Control Center. Just look for the battery icon on there.

Do Not Disturb

It can be rather annoying when a message, FaceTime call or notification awakes you at night, or when your iPhone lights up and emits a noise during an important meeting. These notifications can usually be overridden by simply muting your device or putting it into Airplane mode, but the Do Not Disturb feature is simpler and much more effective.

It works by completely silencing your device between a determined period of time, for example, midnight and 7 AM. During this time, your iPhone won't make a noise, light up or vibrate. You can, however, tell it to allow notifications and calls to still come through from specified contacts.

Enable Do Not Disturb

Swipe up from the bottom to open Control Center, then tap the button near the top that looks like a **crescent moon**. This will instantly enable Do Not Disturb, preventing any calls, messages or notifications from alerting you.

Schedule Do Not Disturb

Let's set a timer, so that Do Not Disturb kicks on at midnight, then finishes at 7 AM. Begin by opening the **Settings** app, then tap the **Do Not Disturb** option.

Set a schedule

Scheduled	
From	22:45
To	07:00

Toggle the Scheduled switch to On. You'll see a From and To field appear below. Tap it, then use the timer wheel to enter the start and end times. In the example above, it's set from 10:45PM to 7 AM. Once entered, tap the button in the top left corner to confirm.

Enable important contacts

If you're expecting an important call, or need to let certain contacts get in touch at all hours, then tap the **Allow Calls From** button. From here you can let anyone call, no one at all, or those in your Favorites list (created in the Contacts app).

Let repeat calls through

Contacts often call repeatedly when they urgently need to get in touch. You can let secondary calls through by toggling the **Repeated Calls** switch to On.

Accessibility Settings

Your iPhone might be an incredibly intuitive device to use, but it's also packed with assistive features that enable people with disabilities to experience and appreciate the usefulness and fun that every iOS devices provides. As a result, those with vision impairments can continue to interact with apps and content, users with hearing aids can enjoy clearer audio, and anyone can use the iPhone's Multi-Touch features, even with just one finger.

Bold text

A handy accessibility feature for those with vision impairments is the Bold Text toggle switch. Once activated, it makes text on the display appear to be bolder. To turn on Bold Text:

1. Open the **Settings** app.
2. Tap **Display & Brightness**.
3. Toggle **Bold Text** on.

Enable button shapes

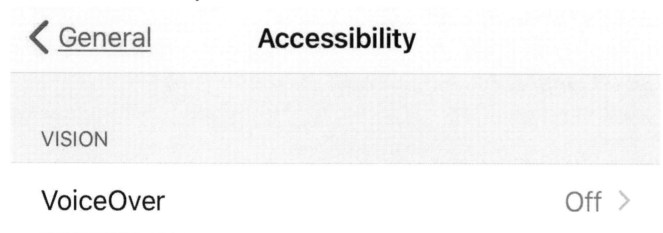

Buttons in iOS don't actually look like buttons. Instead, they're usually a word or short piece of text. To make it more obvious which is a button and which is a piece of information, go to **Settings** > **General** > **Accessibility**, then toggle the **Button Shapes** switch on. This will display thin blue lines beneath buttons, and add small radio buttons to the inside of toggle switches.

Use the LED flash for alerts

LED flash for alerts is intended for anyone with a hearing impairment, but it's also handy for anyone who would like a visual signal when a text message, call or notification comes through; and it works by briefly flashing the LED on the back of the iPhone.

To enable this feature, go to **Settings** > **General** > **Accessibility** then toggle **LED Flash for Alerts** on.

Invert the colors of your screen

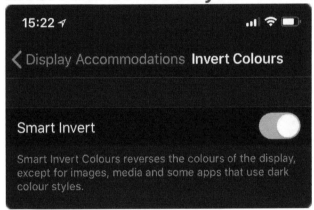

For those with a sensitivity to brightness, the iPhone includes an accessibility feature that inverts every color of the screen. To turn it on, go to **Settings** > **General** > **Accessibility** > **Display Accommodations**. You'll see two options: Smart Invert, and Classic Invert. Smart Invert will reverse the color of everything except images, media and a limited number of apps. Classic Invert will reverse the color of everything on your devices screen.

Enable subtitles and closed captioning

If you'd like to see subtitles and captions for movies, TV shows, podcasts and iTunes U video content purchased from the iTunes Store, then go to **Settings** > **General** > **Accessibility** > **Subtitles & Captioning**, and toggle the top switch on.

Style subtitles and captions

After enabling subtitles (see the previous step), tap the **Style** button to choose from three preset styles. You'll see a preview of each at the top of the screen after selecting one. By tapping **Create New Style** you can customize the font, size, color, background style and text style to suit your taste or requirements.

Adjust the color tint of the display to accommodate for color blindness

Color blindness can be a hassle at the best of times in the real world, and it's a problem that remains when using your device to browse the web, examine photographs or generally interact with the user interface.

Thankfully a built-in accessibility feature can adjust the color palette of the display to accommodate for color blindness, making it possible to see tricky colors in a wide range of spectrums. Here's how it works:

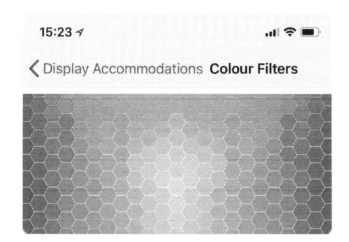

Open the **Settings** app and go to **General** > **Accessibility** > **Display Accommodations** > **Color Filters** then toggle **Color Filters** on.

You'll see a preview of the effect in the graphic at the top of the screen (scroll it left to see two color charts).

To fine tune the color spectrum change, tap the **filters** below the image.

Connect a hearing aid to your iPhone

By connecting a hearing aid with your iPhone you can experience higher quality phone conversations, FaceTime calls and more. Go to **Settings** > **General** > **Accessibility** > **Hearing Aids**, where you can connect to any Bluetooth-enabled hearing aids. Any hearing aids with HAC compatibility (visit support.apple.com/kb/HT4526 to see a list of compatible devices) will also enable you to increase and decrease the volume independently for both ears, monitor battery usage and more.

Change the audio balance

If you're hard of hearing in one ear, or have a faulty pair of headphones, then it's possible to adjust the volume level in either the left or right channels. Go to **Settings** > **General** > **Accessibility**, then scroll down until you see a slide with L on the left side, and R on the right. Drag it left or right to adjust the volume. It might help to play music via the Music app while you make the adjustment.

How to use Assistive Touch

Assistive Touch is a fantastic feature for those with impaired physical and motor skills. It enables you to activate Multi-Touch features such as pinch-to-zoom with only one finger. That's not all, it also enables you to trigger hardware features such as the volume buttons, and even rotate the screen or take a screenshot.

It might sound complicated, but this feature is a doddle to use after a little practice.

Enable Assistive Touch by going to **Settings** > **General** > **Accessibility** > **Assistive Touch**, then toggle the button at the top of the screen.

You'll see a small square button appear on the left side of the screen. By tapping this you can access a window of buttons. Tap on it and you'll see buttons for activating Notification Center, Control Center, Siri, functions on your device, returning to the Home screen and your favorite gestures.

Create an Assistive Touch gesture

From the **Assistive Touch** panel in the **Settings** app, tap the **Create New Gesture** button, then in the light grey window that appears, use two fingers to mimic zooming out of an image. Once you've done, tap the **Save** button at the top of the screen. You'll now see your new gesture saved in the Custom Gestures panel. It's also available in the Favorites section of the shortcuts window.

To use a gesture such as pinch-to-zoom, open the shortcuts panel, tap **Favorites**, then tap your newly created button. You'll see two small arrows appear on-screen. Tap on either one of the arrows, then drag it around the screen. This will replicate a Multi-Touch gesture. This is a really great way to zoom into photos, maps or web pages by using only one finger.

Zoom the screen

The iPhone is designed to be easy for anyone to use, even those with visual impairments. However, there might be occasions where you need to zoom the entire screen. Perhaps the text on a website is too small, or you can't quite make out the detail on an image. Those with visual impairments might also appreciate the ability to zoom the entire screen. Thankfully, using a three-fingered Multi-Touch gesture, it's easy to zoom the screen. You can even specify the zoom from 200 to 500 percent.

Over the page you'll discover how easy it is to zoom and pan your devices screen using just three fingers.

Get Zooming

Go to **Settings** > **General** > **Accessibility**,

then tap the **Zoom** option near the top of the screen. You'll see a toggle switch for enabling screen zoom. Make a note of the text beneath, then toggle the switch. You'll see the screen instantly zoom.

Specify the zoom level

Pan the screen

You can pan the zoomed screen by placing three fingers on the screen then moving them around. Congratulations, now you've learned the basics of zooming the screen, you should never struggle to read small text again!

With the screen zoomed in, images, icons and text are larger and easier to see. You can zoom in and out by double-tapping three fingers on the screen. To specify the exact zoom, **double-tap** with three fingers then slide them up or down the screen. You'll see the zoom level increase or decrease beneath your fingers.

Turn zoom off

Remember, you can turn off the Zoom function at any time by going back into **Settings** > **General** > **Accessibility**, and turning the **Zoom** toggle off.

Use the iPhone camera as a magnifier

If you're struggling to see a small object or piece of text then the magnifier feature in Accessibility lets you use the iPhone's camera as a magnifying glass, effectively letting you zoom in on the world through your iPhone's screen. Here's how to activate the feature:

Go to **Settings** > **General** > **Accessibility** > **Magnifier** then activate it.

Triple-click the **Power** button to turn on the Magnifier.

You can manually zoom the image by using the yellow button, turn on the camera flash for extra light or adjust the brightness and color tones by taping the Filters button in the bottom-left corner.

How to use Speak Selection

Siri is great for setting reminders, opening apps or finding out what's on at the cinema, but you can also use Siri to read out loud selected text, messages and notes.

This feature, called Speak Selection, is particularly useful for those with impaired eyesight, but it's also a fun way to playback text and messages using Siri's voice

To turn Speak Selection on go to **Settings** > **General** > **Accessibility** > **Speech**, then turn on Speak Selection.

To speak words out loud, highlight any text (by double-tapping or tapping and holding on it), then tap the **Speak** button in the pop-up menu. If you can't see the Speak button, tap the small **right arrow** on the pop-up menu and then choose **Speak**.

You can also read Emojis out-loud to make friends and family laugh. To do this just double-tap on the **Emoji** to select it, then ask your device to speak the Emoji out-loud.

Change the voice accent

You can choose from a wide range of voices from the Speech menu. These include Australian accents, British accents, Spanish, Hindi and much more. You can also determine how fast your device reads text by dragging the Speaking Rate slider button.

Speak Screen

This helpful feature is intended for those with vision impairment, and works by reading out-loud all the content that's currently on-screen. To enable Speak Screen, toggle its switch on from the **Speech** panel, then whenever you want to hear what's on-screen just swipe down from the top of the screen with two fingers. A panel will appear that enables you to control speech playback. To close the panel, simply tap the X button.

Highlight words

Notice the **Highlight Words** button? Toggle this switch to see the words highlighted as your device reads them out-loud. Think of Karaoke and you'll get an idea of how this works.

Notification Settings

The iPhone has become the centre of many people's digital lives. As a result, we're constantly bombarded with messages, tweets, updates and notifications. These briefly appear as notifications at the top of the screen, but they're also available to see within Notification Centre, which is accessed by swiping down from the top-left corner of the screen.

Access Notification Settings

It's easy to access the Notifications settings panel, just go to **Settings** > **Notifications**, where you'll be able to customize what notifications and information appear in the Notification Centre screen.

Modify how apps notify you

Swipe down to see a list of apps that display notifications. Select an app (such as Messages), where you'll see a large amount of notifications settings...

Show in Notification Centre

Toggle this switch to enable updates to appear in the Notification Centre (accessed by swiping down from the top of the screen).

Alert Style

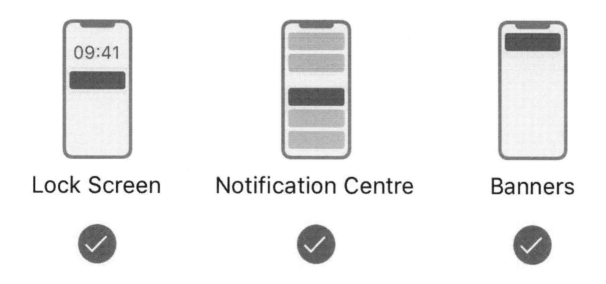

Lock Screen   Notification Centre   Banners

This pane enables you to configure how notifications appear while you're using your iPhone. You'll find three options: **Lock Screen**, **Notification Centre**, and **Banners**. When Lock Screen is selection, any notifications will appear on the lock screen of your device. If Notification Centre is selected, you can also view any notifications by swiping down on the Lock Screen, or down from the top of your device. Finally, if Banners is selected, then alerts will briefly appear at the top of the screen, before disappearing.

Badge app icon

This option enables you to turn off the red numbered badges that appear over app icons when you have a new message or update.

Repeat Alert

iPhone automatically alerts you to new messages twice. You can disable this feature by toggling this switch; or alternatively, tell it to alert you even more times.

View in Lock Screen

Toggle this off to prevent notifications appearing on the lock screen.

Audio Settings

A little personalization can go a long way towards making your iPhone feel like your own device. One of the easiest ways to do this is to alter the sound effects it emits. These include ringtones, email tones, tweet sound effects, calendar alerts, the lock sound and keyboard clicks.

In this chapter, you'll learn how easy it is to select different tones and switch off sound effects that you might not need. You'll also discover how to set an automatic sound check feature, and set a volume limit.

Volume settings

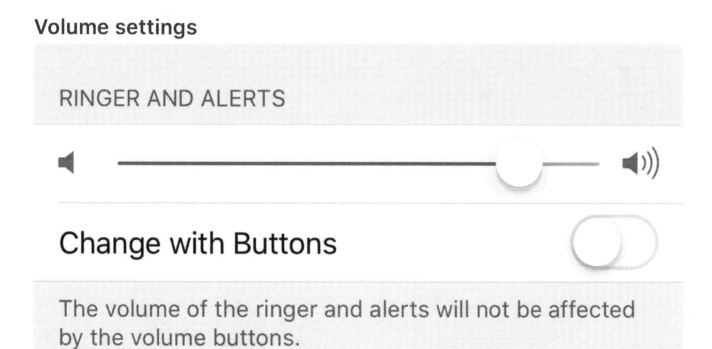

Begin by going to **Settings** > **Sounds & Haptics,** where you'll see a large range of audio options appear on-screen. The slider near the top of the screen enables you to alter the volume level of all sound effects - helpful if you need the device to be quiet, or louder in a busy environment. Toggle the **Change with Buttons** switch to alter the volume of ringtones using the volume buttons on the side of your device.

Change a text/ringtone

The buttons in the centre of the screen enable you to choose from a wealth of sound effects. Choose an option (such as **Text Tone**), then tap on a sound effect to preview and select it.

Disable/enable Lock Sounds

You can disable or enable to lock sound effect by toggling the **Lock Sounds** switch near the bottom of the screen. The lock sound effects are played every time you press the Power button to lock your iPhone.

Turn off keyboard clicks

Your device will automatically emit a keyboard click sound every time you press a key on the on-screen keyboard. You can disable this by toggling the **Keyboard Clicks** switch at the bottom of the screen.

Download new tones

While selecting a new sound effect tone, tap the **Store** button in the top right corner of the screen to find new tones in the iTunes Store. Some are taken from popular music tracks, others are custom sound effects purpose-built for your device.

Change the music equalizer

Go to **Settings** > **Music** > **EQ**. On the following panel you'll be able to choose from a number of equalizer settings. Not all are self-explanatory, so try playing an audio track in the Music app while choosing from the different options. By doing this you can hear how the equalizer affects the playback in real-time.

Set a volume limit

Over time our hearing becomes less sensitive, but it can also be damaged by listening to loud music for long periods of time. To prevent hearing damage, tap the **Volume Limit** button, then lower the setting by dragging the slider button to the left. This will prevent your device from playing music at a volume higher than what is selected.

Stream high-quality music over a cellular data connection

If you really appreciated high-quality audio when listening to music, and don't mind eating into your bandwidth allocation, then it's possible to stream uncompressed music when listening to Apple Music. To do this go to **Settings** > **Music**, then toggle **High Quality on Cellular**.

Enable Sound Check

This clever feature will automatically scan your music files, then set an automatic level that lowers and increases the volume to make tracks and albums sound more coherent across the board. From the **Music** pane in **Settings**, toggle the **Sound Check** switch on to enable this clever feature.

Group album artists together

Sometimes an album can have multiple artists and contributors. From the **Music** pane in the **Settings** app, toggle on **Group By Album Artist** to ensure that all the tracks from multiple artists in retained as one album.

System Updates

Every now and then, the iPhone is updated with new software and features. These might include new Siri features, an extra security setting, battery life improvements or an entirely new mapping system. Updates are free, and usually take minutes to download; and as you're about to find out, they're easy to install.

The Update Badge

There's an easy way to tell when a new software update is available: the Settings app will show a small red badge above it. However, please note that sometimes a software update will still be available but it won't have downloaded to your device. In both cases, the first step is to open the **Settings** app.

Software Updates

From the **Settings** app go to **General** > **Software Update**, you'll see a number alongside it to indicate there's an update available. You'll see a short description of the update. To download and install it, simply tap the **Install Now** button. If the update hasn't automatically downloaded to your device then tap the **Download** and Install button.

The update files will be verified (to make sure that every bit of data has been properly downloaded) then the update will be begin. The process is automated, so sit back while the update installs. After a minute or two your device will restart and return to the Lock Screen. Congratulations, the update has been installed.

Troubleshooting

Most of us will never encounter a serious problem with our iPhone. However, every now and then something might go wrong. Perhaps the battery doesn't last as long as it used too, or maybe a glass of water is spilled over the device. This brief chapter will cover the most common problems, and also explain how to book and attend a Genius Bar appointment.

The Genius Bar

The Genius Bar is a technical support service in every Apple Store where you can get help to solve the problem or receive a replacement device.

They're often referred to as the heart and soul of an Apple Store. Every Genius Bar is manned by a team of technical specialists called "Geniuses". Each has experience solving every kind of hardware and software-related problems. They're also friendly and understanding to boot.

Are the team at the Genius Bar actually geniuses? Ask, and you're likely to receive a shrug, a wink or a bemused look. But these dedicated guys and gals solve even the most complicated problems on a day-to-day basis. If they can't fix a problem with your iPhone then no one else can.

Most services at the Genius Bar are carried out for free. Repairs are carried out in the store, often while you wait. If the Genius can't repair the device on the spot, then a replacement is usually offered.

Booking a Genius Bar appointment

The easiest way to book a Genius Bar appointment is via the Apple Store website. The URL changes depending on your location, but Google search *"Book a Genius Bar appointment"* and the first result will take you to the right page. From the website, you can select your nearest store and choose a suitable time and date – right down to the exact 10 minutes that suit your needs.

Please note that you'll need an Apple ID to book an appointment. This enables the Apple Genius to see your previous software and hardware purchases, which might prove to be helpful when diagnosing problems. It also makes paying for replacements and services much quicker.

Keep in mind that the Genius Bar is a popular service, so the first available appointment might be weeks in advance.

Attending the Genius Bar

Before going to the Genius Bar, make sure to fully backup your device. You can backup your iPhone via iCloud or iTunes on a computer. Both methods save all your apps, text messages, photos, contacts, settings and more. These can be transferred to the new device once it's activated.

If you've never walked into an Apple Store then worry not. They're designed to be easy to understand and navigate. That is if the throngs of crowds aren't in your way. The front of the store is laid out with wooden tables with the most recent devices available to test and play with. Further back you'll see Macs and accessories, and on the back wall is the Genius Bar. If the store is configured in a different way (for example it has multiple rooms/halls), then look for the long wooden bench with black stools in front of it.

You check in with an employee holding a blue iPad. Can't see them through the crowd? Look for any other employee in a blue shirt, they'll be able to help. Alternatively, you can check in using the Apple Store app, but being met face-to-face is always more reassuring.

Once you're at the Genius Bar be polite and explain the problem with your device. The Genius team interview dozens of customers each day, sometimes hundreds. It's likely they've encountered every kind of problem, whether hardware or software related, and should be able to quickly identify what's wrong with a device. Research shows that a smile and positive attitude is the best way to get good customer service, and that applies to both employee and customer. Whereas creating a scene might get you thrown out of the store by security, a friendly chat could get you a free repair or additional advice.

AppleCare+

AppleCare+ provides you with two years of repair or replacement coverage for your iPhone, iPad or iPod touch. This includes two claims of accidental damage or failure of the battery to hold a charge of less than 50% of its original specification. You also get access to telephone technical support. Replacements aren't free, however. You'll need to pay an excess fee of $79, plus applicable tax. Nevertheless, it's still considerably cheaper than replacing the device without AppleCare+, which can cost up to $229.

Other benefits included with AppleCare+ include:

- Mail-in repair. A pre-paid box is posted to your address. Place the device in the box, send it for free and the device will be replaced or fixed.
- Carry-in repair. Take your device into an Apple Store or other Apple Authorized Service Provider and it'll be fixed/replaced on-the-spot.
- Hardware coverage: AppleCare+ also covers the battery, earphones, USB cable and power adapter.

Is AppleCare+ worth it?

This depends from person to person. If you've ever dropped a mobile phone more than once then AppleCare+ might be a good idea. Similarly, if your household is shared by children or pets than you might want to look into buying technical support. Those who enjoy wild parties on a regular occasion might also want to buy the extra coverage. But if you're the sort who buys a case and keeps the device within reach at all times, then it's unlikely you'll ever need AppleCare+. Instead, it offers peace of mind and reassurance.

Water damaged iPhone?

Water is usually a death sentence for electronic devices. That's because water conducts electricity, passing it instantly from one component to another causing them to overload. Impure water (such as fizzy drinks or sea water) also contains impurities that bind to electronics and corrode them. These impurities stay in the device even when it's dried, causing further damage over time.

Thankfully, the iPhone XS and XS Max are water protected from liquids to an IP68 rating. That means you can drop your iPhone into a liquid of two meters deep, for up to 30-minutes, and not see any damage to the internal components. If your iPhone sinks any deeper, or stays in liquid for a considerable amount of time, then you might be in trouble. Water damage typically causes the speakers and microphone to fail, can cause dark shadows to appear on the screen, or can break the device entirely. If you suspect this has happened, then it's a good idea to take your iPhone to the nearest Apple Genius Bar for repair or replacement.

It's worth noting that every iPhone and iPad includes a liquid damage indicator. This is a small strip inside the Lightning Bolt port that changes color on contact with water. The Genius uses this strip to detect the presence of water when identifying problems with a device. So if you've dropped your iPhone into very deep water there's little point pretending otherwise at the Genius Bar!

Don't turn on a wet electronic device!

If you've accidentally dunked your iPhone into liquid then you're probably okay to keep using as normal. Just blow it dry and hope for the best. If it has been in liquid overnight, then do the opposite! Don't blow into it or shake the device, because if water has leaked into the casing this will only move it around and potentially cause further problems.

The best way to dry a wet device

First of all, avoid any heat sources. Hairdryers are hot enough to melt the solder inside an iPhone. Similarly, avoid other heaters or sources of fire. Room temperature is your friend. The most efficient way to dry a wet device is to place it in a sealed container with silica gel packets. These are the same gels you find packaged with most large electrical devices. They typically come in small paper sachets. If you don't have gel packets to hand, then white rice has been known to work. It's highly advisable to leave the device encased in rice for 24 hours, before repeating the process with a second portion of rice. Be patient, the longer you can leave the device to dry the more likely it will still work when it's turned back on. Good luck!

Cracked Screen

If you've never dropped an iPhone then consider yourself lucky, for the sickening sound of glass and metal hitting a hard surface will make any stomach drop. It doesn't matter how strong a piece of glass is – it can, and will, break under certain conditions. Glass is particularly prone to knocks around edges and corners. On the iPhone it's common to see breaks emanate outwards from the lock/mute button.

iPhone uses Gorilla Glass for the construction of its screen. Gorilla Glass is created through a proprietary process that sees raw materials being blended into a glass composition that's microns thick. A chemical strengthening process then sees large ions being "stuffed" into the glass surface, before the glass is placed in a hot bath of molten salt at 400°. Needless to say, it's a complicated process that results in the strongest glass available in a consumer product. The process is refined and improved every few years, resulting in stronger versions of the glass that are subsequently manufactured into the latest devices. iPhone XS used Gorilla Glass 6, which is claimed to be 40% more scratch-resistant than earlier iterations.

Cracked screens are incredibly dangerous and should be fixed immediately. The fine cracks in Gorilla Glass will cut skin on contact, and it's possible that small pieces will fall out causing further problems. So, what's the best course of action when the glass screen on your iPhone device is broken?

AppleCare+

If you've already purchased AppleCare+ then congratulations, because a replacement screen for your device will cost you an excess fee of $29, plus applicable tax. If you've already broken the screen and wish to buy AppleCare+ then you're out of luck.

Take the device to an Apple Store

The price of replacing a screen differs from one device to another. Older devices use separate components for the glass and LCD, whereas recent devices include composite screens that merge the LCD with the glass. This improves color reproduction and reduces glare, but increases repair costs. Here's a quick breakdown of the screen replacement costs:

- iPhone 6, iPhone SE: $129
- iPhone 8, iPhone 7, iPhone 6s, iPhone 6 Plus: $149
- iPhone 8 Plus, iPhone 7 Plus, iPhone 6s Plus: $169

- iPhone X: $279

Take the device to a third-party

Typically, you can take your iPhone to a third-party repair shop and get it fixed for anywhere between $30 to $99. Expect the repair to take around 30 minutes. Afterwards you'll have a brand new screen that's scratch and smash free. Be aware, however, that it's likely you'll see cuts and chips in the frame around the screen. This is a consequence of the repair shop having to force-off the screen by hand.

Other Problems

It's rare, but sometimes hardware buttons stop responding or become stuck. Perhaps the Power button no longer clicks or the volume buttons stop working.

If your device is less than a year old, or covered by AppleCare+, then a replacement is free. If older than a year expect to pay a replacement fee. Make an appointment with the Genius Bar to find out, or alternatively, try using the Assistive Touch accessibility feature (see Settings chapter for more information.) This enables you to trigger hardware buttons via touch-screen controls.

If your iPhone has completely frozen and refuses to respond to taps or hardware buttons, then there are three solutions you can attempt:

Force quit an app

If an app stops working, freezes or acts up, just swipe up from the bottom of the screen, then stop halfway to access the multitasking window. Next, slide the app which has crashed, up off the screen. This will force-quit the app and remove it from the iPhone's temporary memory.

Force restart the device

Sometimes your iPhone might stop responding to touch. This is very rare, but it does happen from time-to-time. It might be an app that causes the problem, or a conflict within the operating system. In these extreme cases you can force the device to restart. To do this hold both the **Power** button and the **down volume** button simultaneously for between five and 10 seconds. When the iPhone restarts you can let go.

Let the battery run dry

If the hardware buttons are stuck or broken, then simply let the battery run dry. Note that this might take up to 10 hours.

How to erase and restore an iPhone via recovery mode

This is a bit drastic, so only perform a wipe and restore if the Apple logo has been stuck on-screen for more than 10 minutes. Here's how it's done:

1. Plug your iPhone into a Mac or PC with iTunes running.
2. Turn off your iPhone if it isn't already (you might need to force restart it).
3. Press and hold the **power** button for 3 seconds.
4. While holding down the power button, press and hold the **volume down** button, and keep them pressed down for 10 seconds.
5. Let go of the **power** button but keep holding the **volume down** button for about 5 seconds (if you see the Plug into iTunes screen you've held it too long).
6. If the screen stays black then you've done it - your iPhone is now ready to restore using iTunes.

Back up your iPhone to iTunes

Your iPhone will automatically back itself up to iCloud every time it's plugged in and connected to Wi-Fi, but nevertheless it's still a good idea to have a local backup on your Mac or PC in case of emergencies. Here's how to fully backup your iPhone with iTunes on a desktop computer:

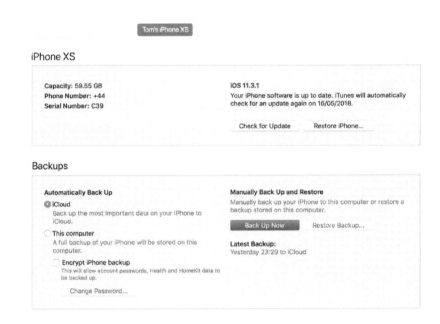

1. Plug iPhone into your Mac or PC.
2. Launch iTunes if it doesn't automatically open.
3. If a message asks for your iPhone's passcode, or to Trust This Computer, follow the onscreen steps.
4. Click on the **iPhone** icon in the menu bar, then click on the **Summary** tab.
5. Look for the Backups box. Where it says Manually Backup and Restore, click **Back Up Now**.
6. A local backup will now be created and saved to your computer.

Restore your iPhone from an iTunes backup

If you're having problems with your iPhone then reverting to a local backup is a fairly straightforward process. Here's how it works:

1. Open iTunes on your Mac or PC then connect your iPhone using a Lightning cable.
2. If a message asks for your iPhone's passcode, or to Trust This Computer, follow the onscreen steps.
3. Click on the iPhone icon in the menu bar, then look for the Backups field in the Summary tab.

4. Select **Restore Backup**, then choose the relevant backup if there are more than one saved.

5. Click Restore, then wait for the process to finish. You may be asked to enter the password for your backup if it's encrypted.

What to do if you lose your iPhone

First of all, don't panic! It's probably somewhere obvious, like down the side of your sofa or in your jacket pocket. If you've looked around and still can't find it then there are a few things you can try...

Call it

Sounds obvious, right? Just use another iPhone or landline to call your iPhone and listen out for the ringtone.

Use your Apple Watch

If you're wearing your Apple Watch check to see if it's still connected to your iPhone. If it's not connected you'll see a small red iPhone icon at the top of the screen. If it is connected then your iPhone isn't far away.

Next, swipe up from the bottom of your Apple Watch screen to access Control Centre, then tap the iPhone **Alert icon** (it looks like the iPhone with curved lines on either side). After a second or two, your iPhone will emit a loud noise - even if it's in Silent mode.

Use Find My iPhone

Use another device or computer and go to www.icloud.com. Try to log in. If two-factor authentication is enabled and you're asked for a passcode, use your Mac or iPad to get the code and enter it. If you don't have another iOS device or Mac, it's time to call Apple for further help.

Once you're logged into iCloud click the **Find iPhone** icon, then wait for your devices to load. Next, click on your iPhone via the Map screen, or click the drop-down icon at the top of the screen and select it. In the pop-up panel, you'll be able to play a sound, erase your iPhone or place it into Lock Mode.

Track your iPhone in Lost Mode

If Lost Mode is enabled while your iPhone is turned on and Location Services were activated then you'll be able to immediately track its location via the map screen. If Location Services were disabled when you turned on Lost Mode, then it's temporarily turned on to help you track the device. If your iPhone was turned off completely, then Lost Mode will activate when it's next turned on and you'll be able to track it then.

Erase your iPhone

If the worst has happened and you don't think you'll be able to get your iPhone back, then you can securely erase its contents to prevent someone from accessing your data. When erased an activation lock is enabled and Find My iPhone is automatically turned on. This means if your iPhone is ever restored by someone else you can still track it and be assured that they can't unlock it without your Apple ID and password.

After you've selected Erase iPhone:

- If it's online then your iPhone will be immediately erased, and you'll get a confirmation email to let you know.
- If it's offline then it will be erased when it's next turned on If you manage to find your iPhone before it's turned on then you can cancel the erase by logging into iCloud, selecting your iPhone then choosing Stop Erase Request.
- If it's erased and then you find it, you can restore the most recent backup from iCloud during the set-up process.

Glossary

Although this book has been written as concisely as possible and is jargon-free, there might be some words or phrases that you don't understand. Where's that's the case, this glossary should help.

A

Accessibility
A series of features build into iOS intended to help those with impairments make the most of their iPhone. You can find the Accessibility features in the Settings app.

AirPlay
A feature which enables users to stream audio and video from one Apple device to another. For example, by using AirPlay it's possible to open a YouTube video, then stream it directly to an AppleTV.

App
Short for 'application', an app is a piece of software designed for a particular task, such as creating graphics or writing letters. Your iPhone comes with several apps pre-installed, such as Safari, which lets you browse the web; and Pages, which lets you create documents.

App Store
This is an app pre-installed on your iPhone which lets you purchase and download additional apps.

Apple ID
This is the name of an account registered with Apple. It is used to purchase content from the App Store, iTunes Store, and to log into iCloud.

B

Bluetooth
A wireless technology used to transfer data from one device to another. Bluetooth is most often used for wireless headphones, keyboards and fitness trackers.

Browser
The name of an app which lets you access websites on the internet. Your iPhone comes with Apple's Safari browser, but others are available to download from the App Store.

D

Dock

This refers to the collection of app shortcuts at the bottom of the Home screen on your iPhone. It's fully customizable, so you can add and remove apps, or rearrange them.

E

Emoticon / Emojis

A small drawing used to express an emotion or say something with an image, instead of a word. Typically they are depicted as yellow faces, but there are literately hundreds of emoticons covering food, vehicles, events, and animals.

F

FaceTime

Think of FaceTime as video and audio calling from one Apple device to another. It works over the internet, so it's free too.

Folder

Think of a folder as a box of files. You can keep as many files inside a folder, plus other folders too. You'll find folders of apps on the Home screen of your iPhone, or within the Files app.

G

Gestures

Actions performed with your fingers on the iPhone screen. These include using two fingers to pinch-to-zoom, or a swipe sideways to go 'backward' or 'forward' through apps.

I

iCloud

The collective name for Apple's online services. Using iCloud you can store files or a backup of your entire iPhone on Apple's servers, download apps and music, or sync content between all of your Apple devices.

iOS

The name of Apple's mobile operating system used on iPhone and iPad.

iTunes

This is the app used to play and download music, film, TV and podcasts.

L

Lightning

The cable used by iPhone, iPad and many

Apple accessories. It's used to power and recharge these devices.

Link

This is simply a link to a website or document on the internet. It's usually represented by blue text within a document or web page.

M

Mail

The application on your iPhone used to send, receive and read emails.

N

Notification Center

This is a small panel on your iPhone which lists all your recent notifications, messages and updates. You can also access widgets from here, which let you perform simple tasks like calculation. You can access Notification Center by swiping from the left on the Home screen.

P

Photos

An app on your iPhone which stores all of your photos and syncs them across all of your devices.

S

Safari

An app on your iPhone for accessing websites. If you have a Mac or iPad then you can also share bookmarks between devices.

Siri

A virtual assistant on your iPhone. You can talk to Siri and ask questions, get weather reports and interact with features on your iPhone.

Spotlight

This is a search engine for your iPhone. You can use Spotlight to search for files, apps, and features. You can also search the web for weather results, stocks and other search queries.

T

Tab

A tab is a view of a website within Safari. You can have multiple tabs within one window, making easy to keep several websites open at once.

Touch ID
The name of the fingerprint sensor on the right-side of the Touch Bar. By using Touch ID you can log into your Mac or make purchases using only your fingerprint.

U

URL
An URL is an address for a website. For example, www.apple.com is the URL used to access Apple's website.

W

Wi-Fi
A wireless method for accessing the internet.

Widgets
These are small panels which let you perform simple tasks like check the weather, see stock updates or perform a calculation. You can find widgets in the Notification Center.

Thanks for reading

So, you've come to the end of the book. Hopefully you've discovered a trick or two that will help you to really make the most of your iPhone XS.

If you would like to get in touch, have tips of your own, or have spotted a problem, please send an email via **mail@tapguides.co.uk**

Book Updates

iOS is constantly updated with new features, security patches and improvements. This book will be updated regularly to reflect these updates and changes.

Here's how to make sure you never miss out on these key changes and additions:

If you bought the ebook on Amazon:

The Kindle edition will atomically update on your device when a new version is available. If you have disabled automatic updates:

1. Go to **Manage Your Content and Devices**.
2. Select the **Settings** tab.
3. Under **Automatic Book Update**, select **On**.
4. Note: If you select Off, you will no longer receive book updates automatically.

If you book the print edition
If you bought this book in print then you are entitled to download the eBook version for free. Just head over the Kindle MatchBook (use Google if you don't know the link), log in and your free download should appear near the top of the page.